EGYPTIAN·*B*OOKSHELF

DISEASE

Joyce Filer

University of Texas Press
Austin

International Standard Book Number 0–292–72498–5
Library of Congress Catalog Card Number 95–61447

Text Copyright © 1995 Trustees of the British Museum

Designed by Grahame Dudley Associates

Front cover: The coffin and skeletal remains of a child with 'brittle bone' disease.

Frontispiece: X-rays are useful in detecting disease or trauma. This X-ray of the skull
of Tutankhamun does not indicate any cranial disease.

EGYPTIAN·BOOKSHELF

DISEASE

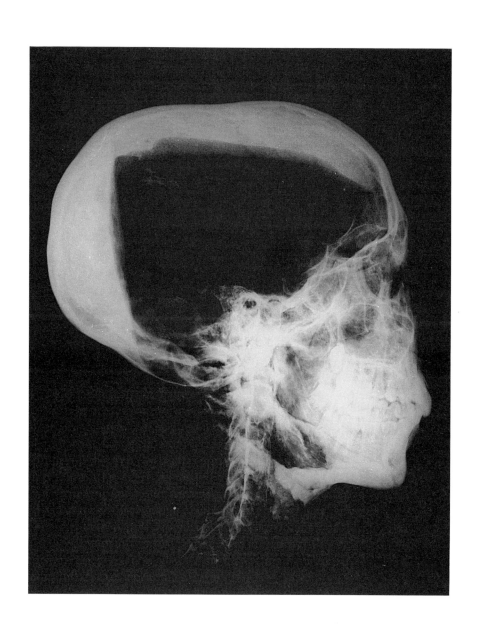

Contents

Acknowledgements

I would like to thank Professor Don Brothwell for reading a draft copy of the text and offering comments and suggestions. Carol Andrews, John Taylor, Richard Parkinson and Stephen Quirke read drafts and offered extensive comments and corrections. I would like to thank Jeffrey Spencer for valuable discussion and advice concerning sources of artistic evidence and John Taylor for information about Horemkenesi. Any errors remaining are, of course, my responsibility.

I am very grateful to the following: Joann Fletcher, Manchester University, for providing information about aspects of hair from ancient Egypt and for allowing me to use her photographs of an ancient head louse and the Seneb family group; Dr R Foley, Duckworth Laboratory, Cambridge for allowing me to examine and photograph skulls from Kerma and Giza; Professor F Hussein, National Research Centre, Cairo for allowing me to examine the skeletons of the dwarfs Perenankh and the female from the workmen's community at Giza who died in childbirth (chapter 4); Angela Thomas, Bolton Museum and Art Gallery, for allowing me to examine the biological material in her care and for providing information and photographs; Dr M Schultz, Göttingen University, for allowing me to use his comments on the 'Junker teeth' (chapter 7) and Corinne Duhig, Wolfson College, Cambridge for allowing me to use information from her study re-examining tooth surfaces. I would also like to thank the field directors of the British Institute in Eastern Africa and the Sudan Archaeological Research Society for permission to include information about the Soba and Gabati excavations.

The following also supplied photographs and/or information: Carol Andrews, Jonathan Musgrave, Bettina Schmitz, Stephen Hughes, Geoffrey T Martin, Rosalie David, Eddie Tapp, Martin Davies and the Egypt Exploration Society, to them I am most grateful. Thanks are due to Naomi Mott, Reg Davis and Rodney Reznek who provided radiographic images. The photography of British Museum objects was mostly undertaken by Janet Peckham to whom I would like to offer my thanks. The drawings of the Queen of

Punt and the stele of Roma are by Richard Parkinson and the map is by Claire Thorne, my thanks are due to them. All other figures were drawn by Neville Parker.

I would like to thank my editors Sarah Derry and Carolyn Jones for their advice and guidance.

For their support and encouragement I would like to thank the following: W Vivian Davies; Roxie Walker; Richard Barritt and Bunny; Margaret Serpico; Lesley Hannigan and Tony Legge (Department of Extra-Mural Studies, Birkbeck College) and Naomi Mott (Institute of Archaeology, London). Thanks are due to Tania Watkins and Cathy Limb and to Pat Terry, Jackie Casey and Jane Johnson who at various times were involved in typing the text.

Above all I would like to thank my friend Neville Parker for his hard work drawing the figures and for his support and encouragement. I dedicate this book to him.

AUTHOR'S NOTE

In writing an introductory book on the vast subject of the health status of the ancient Egyptians it is inevitable that there will be omissions. The book aims to concentrate on the range of health problems encountered in Egypt and Nubia and where possible indications of the effects on daily life are given. A specific chapter on doctors and treatment has not been included; this subject will be more fully treated in John Nunn's forthcoming book (in press at the time of writing). Whilst providing an overview of current knowledge about the health of the ancient Egyptians and Nubians this book also offers the opportunity to examine some new material from recent excavations in Egypt and those undertaken by the Sudan Archaeological Research Society.

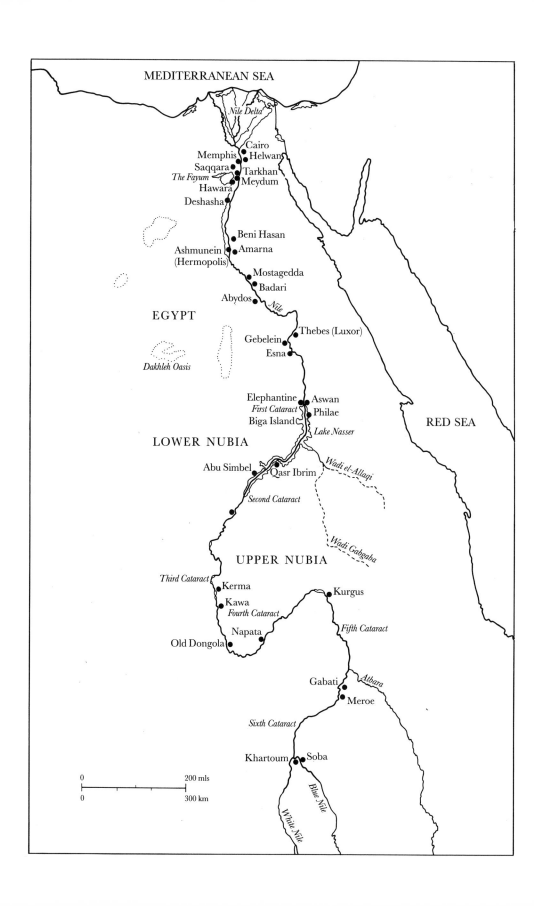

MEDITERRANEAN SEA

Nile Delta

Cairo
Memphis Helwan
Saqqara Tarkhan
The Fayum Meydum
Hawara
Deshasha

Beni Hasan
Ashmunein Amarna
(Hermopolis)
Mostagedda
Badari
Abydos *Nile*

EGYPT

Thebes (Luxor)
Gebelein
Esna

Dakhleh Oasis

Elephantine Aswan
First Cataract Philae
Biga Island *Lake Nasser*

LOWER NUBIA

Abu Simbel Qasr Ibrim *Wadi el-Allaqi*

Second Cataract

Wadi Gabgaba

UPPER NUBIA

Third Cataract Kermā Kurgus
Kawa
Fourth Cataract
Old Dongola Napata *Fifth Cataract*

Gabati *Atbara*
Meroe

Sixth Cataract

Khartoum Soba

Blue Nile

White Nile

RED SEA

| 0 | | 200 mls |
| 0 | | 300 km |

CHAPTER ONE

The Environment

The lives of ancient Egyptians were shaped by the environment around them, both for the good and for the bad. The land, the river and the climate were of great benefit to the people but in certain circumstances they produced hazards to health and promoted disease and sickness. Other important environmental factors such as diet and nutrition also affected the state of health of the ancient Egyptians, as did social factors such as housing, hygiene and sanitation and the occupations they engaged in.

Egypt has a remarkable landscape. On either side of the River Nile run relatively narrow strips of land which provided the fertile fields for growing crops. The ancient Egyptians called this land Kemet, the 'Black Land', after the dark alluvial silt which enriched it. Bordering the other sides of the cultivated areas were the tawny-red desert lands which they called Deshret, the 'Red Land'. The Egyptians buried their dead in the dry ground to help preserve the bodies in order not to waste any of the precious agricultural land.

The Greek author Strabo, writing during the first century BC, tells us that any visitors to Egypt were informed of the importance of the Nile by the natives before learning anything else about their great civilisation. Even today we can witness the central part the Nile plays in daily life. In ancient Egypt, between July and October each year, the Nile flooded its banks depositing a rich and fertile layer of alluvial silt onto the land. Thus it may be said that the Nile created Egypt by building up layers of soil. The early agriculture of Egypt relied on natural irrigation and drainage of the land. Butzer suggests that by the end of the Predynastic era there had been a transition to an artificial system of irrigation whereby the flood waters were diverted

1 *Modern Egypt: a fellah (peasant) prepares his fields for planting seeds.*

to nourish those areas not normally reached by the inundation, increasing the area of fertile land. In the Delta, 'turtlebacks', large sand islands, provided land for settlements. Today, following the construction of the Aswan dams, the Nile waters are controlled, and cannot flood, eliminating the yearly uncertainty over the level of the flood waters which so preoccupied the ancient Egyptian, for the amount of water dictated whether or not the people ate.

The agricultural year began in earnest when the waters receded and seeds were planted. It is difficult not to agree with Aristotle's statement that the Nile was highly productive and nourishing, for in successful seasons the land and the Nile together could produce not only an adequate supply of food for the populace but also a substantial surplus useful for storage and trade. Yet there were times when the Nile flooded either too little or too much, causing damage and over-saturation of the soil and resulting in crop failure and periods of famine and nutritional stress. Reliefs from the Old Kingdom show the serious effects of famine at a time when the flood waters failed to reach the necessary level. Although exaggerating for dramatic effect, the pessimistic literature of the Middle Kingdom period implies the inadequate inundation levels causing famine and describes the consequence of low floods among the catalogue of social ills. In *The Prophecy of Neferti*, 'the sage laments that the river of Egypt is dry, so that water is crossed on foot; water will be sought for ships to sail'. Following a successful inundation, however, the fertile land could produce luxuriant vegeta-

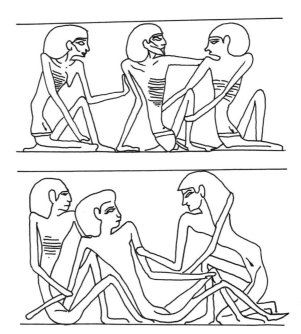

2 *Famine victims depicted on the causeway leading to the pyramid of King Wenis (Fifth Dynasty, Saqqara). People, who may be foreigners, are starving to death, their faces drawn and their bodies emaciated.*

tion and a large variety of foodstuffs and these, together with various dietary problems, will be discussed later in this section.

The Nile was a focal point in Egyptian life, providing drinking water, washing facilities and a means of travel and transport. In ancient as well as in modern times the tasks of fetching water and washing clothes offered the opportunity for neighbours to gather together. Clothes would be washed in the Nile waters and pots of water would be carried home for cooking and drinking. Unfortunately, this close and constant contact with the Nile also allowed contact with the endoparasites harboured in its waters.

In modern reports from Egypt the disease schistosomiasis has been described as one of the most prominent public health hazards affecting both the physical and mental development of children and adults and it is likely that the disease had an important part to play in ancient times. *Schistosoma haematobia*, the parasitic worm which causes the disease, has a complex life cycle which involves using the water snail as an intermediary host. The worm begins its life when eggs are released into the human bloodstream. These ova produce a chemical which destroys areas of the bloodstream's surface through which they gain access to the intestines and the bladder from where they move into the outside world. Normally, the ova must land in fresh water in order to develop into larvae, but the host water snails can survive in a variety of habitats, including standing water in the Egyptian basin irrigation system. They then locate and enter water snails and remain there until fully developed. The larvae then seek human hosts and the cycle is repeated. During their journey through the human body the worms cause much damage and discomfort.

Schistosomiasis, also known as bilharzia, is probably a disease of great antiquity. The Ebers Papyrus devotes two columns to the treatment and prevention of blood in the urine – one of the standard symptoms of schistosomiasis. The existence of these worms in antiquity was confirmed by Ruffer earlier this century when he identified calcified ova in the kidneys of two Twentieth Dynasty mummies. During the examination of Nakht, a mummy in Toronto, it was found that this adolescent Egyptian male was infested by schistosoma and tapeworms and it is likely that this double parasitic burden contributed to the young man's early death. To date, the earliest evidence for schistosomiasis has been found in an adolescent, predynastic, naturally dessicated body in the British Museum (plate I). Tests on a sample of skin from this young person have revealed an active infection at the time of death and this has prompted questions about the subsequent history of the disease. Various scenes from ancient Egyptian tombs show people wading in water, often whilst herding cattle, thus illustrating the ease with which the schistosoma worm can find a human host. Infestation by these worms could lead to anaemia – due to loss of blood – resulting in tiredness and in extreme cases, death.

Another parasite present in Egyptian waters also contributed to ill health. The guinea worm (*Dracunculus mediensis*) enters the body in an immature form in drinking water, and develops in the stomach. Later the worm burrows into the abdominal wall to mate. The guinea worm can move to any part of the human body but the pregnant female prefers to settle in the legs where the resulting irritation causes an ulcer through which she lays her eggs. Upon reaching water these eggs infect more people. The guinea worm requires a dry climate and so is well suited to the climates of India, Arabia and of course, Egypt. As the worm can grow up to four feet in length it can cause great pain, especially if it has moved near the joints and it is in these areas that any resulting skeletal changes may be detected. A mummy in Manchester Museum, No. 1770, examined by the Manchester mummy team in the 1970s, contained a calcified male guinea worm. At one time it was suggested that this thirteen-year-old child had her legs amputated because of guinea worm infestation, but this now seems unlikely. Although we cannot ascertain absolutely the extent of endoparasitic infection in ancient populations, the modern data suggest that the condition is still widespread. Certainly the implications for ancient Egyptians is that these parasites were responsible for much ill health and even death.

As already stated, one of the benefits of the River Nile was the ease of travel and transport. Throughout Egyptian history the river was a unifying force providing a link between Upper and Lower Egypt. Travel on the Nile was facilitated by a current flowing from the south and winds blowing from the north and so advantage could be taken of the elements in either direction. From the health point of view this meant that foodstuffs could be transported quickly from one town to another along the Nile thus lessening the chances of being spoiled. Of course meat being transported over long distances would have been preserved using salt. Salt, available from several areas in Egypt, preserves by extracting water from the animal tissues immersed in it. The resulting dehydrated meat, poultry or fish would then be immune to bacterial attack. Such preserved and easily portable foods were invaluable sources of nutrition for people on long journeys such as soldiers, traders and travellers. Efficient transportation also meant that people could enjoy a wider choice of foods to supplement their local produce.

Very importantly for the Egyptian diet, the Nile and the Red Sea yielded a variety of fish, many of which are represented in tomb decorations. Meat was beyond the means of most ancient Egyptians and doubtless the growth from predynastic times of an efficient fishing industry was prompted by a need for a cheaper form of protein. Fishing provided a high yield of produce for the amount of time and manpower expended and so fish became an economical staple of the ancient Egyptian diet, either fresh or dried and salted, although it remained forbidden for certain members of society.

In Book II (75) of his Histories, Herodotus stated his opinion that the health of the ancient Egyptians was due to the lack of variability in the weather. The climate in Egypt, however, worked both for and against its inhabitants. On the one hand the sun's rays provided nourishment for the body in the form of vitamin D and this may have helped prevent rickets. Yet on the other hand the intense heat encouraged flies and other insects which spread infection from dirt and rubbish to humans. Flies then, as today, were responsible for many eye infections. One type of infection was trachoma (an inflammation of the inner surface of the eye lids) which often led to blindness. Some of the medical papyri give advice for the treatment of a number of eye complaints. Some tomb illustrations suggest that some of those who were blind were employed as musicians. In an emotional letter from the Nineteenth Dynasty, the draftsman Pay begs his son not to neglect him for he is 'in darkness' (i.e. blind) and he asks his son to bring him treatment for his eyes in the form of honey, ochre and genuine galena. Apart from encouraging flies, the heat no doubt caused minor complaints such as heatstroke, headaches and sunburn. Many tomb paintings show farmers at work semi-clad and without head coverings, and while these may not be altogether realistic, they suggest that the people were well acclimatised to such working conditions.

In Lower Egypt the climate promoted an additional health hazard. As the inundation waters receded dark marshy areas appeared providing the ideal conditions for breeding mosquitoes and consequently for the spread of malaria. The devastating effect of malaria on earlier Mediterranean societies (in particular the Greek colonies) has been widely discussed but the extent of malaria in ancient Egypt has been far from clear. In Herodotus (Book ii, 94) it is stated that the marsh-country (i.e. Lower Egypt) was infested by gnats and that the people slept under nets to avoid them. It is possible that Herodotus meant mosquitoes, and recent scientific developments strongly suggest that some mummies from ancient Egypt were infected with malaria. This will be discussed in Chapter 5.

From time to time the Sahara winds blew up dust storms and during their daily lives the people could not avoid breathing sand into their mouths and lungs, resulting in chest infections, blocked sinuses and headaches. Evidence from some mummies shows that some people developed pneumoconiosis after sand particles had entered the lungs. In this condition the lungs become inflamed and the affected person has difficulty in breathing. Evidence for this condition was found in PUM ii, the mummy of a thirty-five- to forty-year-old man belonging to Philadelphia Museum of Art, and in several mummies examined by the Manchester mummy team. To reduce the effects of the sun's glare men and women wore eye paint. One type was made from green malachite and was called *wadju*, the other which was more frequently used was called *mesdemet* and was made from galena or stibnite. Apart from protecting the eyes from the sun and being decorative, galena (or black eye paint) had some medicinal properties. Some Egyptian medical papyri recommend *mesdemet* for eye problems and, as we have read, the blind draftsman Pay requested 'genuine galena' for its curative effects.

Ancient Egyptians wore linen garments made from locally grown flax. This was a healthy response to the prevailing climate as the loosely woven fibres allowed the skin to breathe, preventing the build-up of bacteria from perspiration. Men working outdoors were generally shown wearing a short kilt-like garment without a covering for the upper torso and as noted previously they were unlikely to be affected by the sun's intense rays. As women ideally tended to work indoors (though farmers' wives helped with the harvest) their complexions were represented as paler and they usually wore garments which covered most of the body. Herodotus (Book ii, 37) noted that the Egyptians washed their linen frequently which was essential considering the 'stickiness' of the climate. In their quest for cleanliness Herodotus also tells us that the priests shaved their bodies every other day to prevent lice infestation and evidence from mummies indicates that certainly some of the wealthier members of society shaved their heads and wore wigs. This was probably done for comfort in the hot climate but may also have been an attempt to be rid of head lice. That this latter purpose was not always successful has been shown by Strouhal's report of lice eggs on the hair of the weaver Nakht during the autopsy of his body in Toronto in 1974. G. Armelagos and colleagues also found adult lice on Nubian bodies dated to the 4th–6th centuries BC. More recently research undertaken by J. Fletcher at the Manchester Museum has brought to light the earliest sample of lice so far found on ancient Egyptian hair, of early dynastic date.

Contrary to popular belief nits (and the adult lice) are not proof of poor hygiene, but rather the opposite. Head lice cannot travel on greasy or dirty hair shafts and so their presence on Egyptian hair would support the observation by Herodotus that the Egyptians were indeed very concerned with cleanliness. Apart from the discomfort, lice (on the hair or body) may cause dermatitis from scratching and more seriously they may carry epidemic typhus or relapsing fever. The prevalence of such diseases is difficult to determine as they leave no evidence on skeletons.

The climate – hot and dry with occasional dust storms – influenced the design of housing in Egypt. The richer members of society had more spacious and better appointed houses, yet overall the main aim for all classes was to minimise the effects of the climate on daily living.

The evidence for Egyptian housing comes from a variety of sources. Housing representing different levels of society has been found at Amarna (ancient Akhetaten) an Eighteenth Dynasty site in Middle Egypt which is currently being excavated by Dr B. J. Kemp. Here the villa-like houses of the top members of society had a central living area and other important functional rooms at ground level. Some of these better houses had planned sanitation facilities. In some cases a stone or wooden seat with a keyhole-shaped opening served as a latrine with a removable bowl for waste underneath. One house had a bathing area with stone slabs forming the base and splashback for a shower. Water would be poured over the bather from a jug with waste water draining away through an outlet in the wall. At the other end of the social scale a workmen's village on the eastern side of Akhetaten has revealed houses crowded together with a limited amount of light and space. Such living conditions may have led to ill health. Tuberculosis thrives in such conditions and parasitic infections are easily passed on.

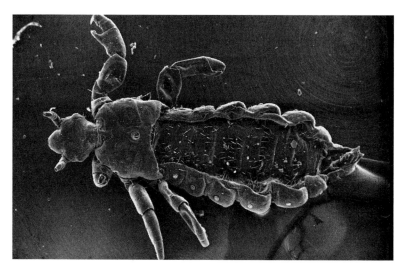

3 *An adult head louse (c.2 mm in length) found by J. Fletcher in a sample of human hair from Abydos, c.3,000 BC. It is remarkably similar to its modern counterpart.*

Deir el-Medina is a workmen's village situated in the cliffs opposite Luxor (ancient Thebes). The houses were of a similar design throughout the village, any variations depending on the wealth and status of the owner. The average, one-storeyed house had three or four rooms and appears to have had a reasonable amount of space and light but, as with the houses of the workmen at Akhetaten, we do not know how many people actually lived in them. Some houses at Deir el-Medina had areas for storing food and a stairway leading from the courtyard to the roof. Whilst Deir el-Medina presents less grand living conditions than the villa-like houses at Amarna, it should be stressed that these workmen, building tombs for royalty, were still privileged and their houses are unlikely to represent those of the ordinary person.

Domestic buildings were built of sun-baked bricks made from the alluvial mud left behind after the annual inundation. The mud was mixed with Nile water and, to increase the strength of the bricks, a vegetable matter (often straw) was added. After being shaped in moulds the bricks where then left to dry in the sun. The bricks were readily available and cheap, enabling houses to be altered and

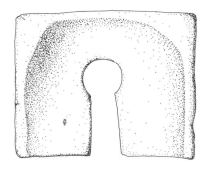

4 *Keyhole shaped seat of wood or stone, fitted over a removable bowl, which served as a lavatory in some higher class houses at Amarna. Eighteenth Dynasty.*

repaired easily. Unfortunately, working in mud and water increased the labourer's chances of becoming infected with the types of parasites described above. Mud-brick buildings were durable and because of the Egyptian climate, were unlikely to be damaged by storms. From the health point of view these houses retained warmth and gave protection from the intense heat of the sun but inadequate ventilation caused by smoking fires took its toll on weaker individuals. Excavations at Amarna have revealed smoke-blackened roof timbers recording a heavy passage of soot. Such an atmosphere would surely have contributed to the condition known as anthracosis when smoke inhalation results in carbon particles settling in lung tissue. It is no wonder there are recipes in magical texts designed to freshen the house. Another purpose of these concoctions was to fumigate houses to rid them of vermin. Warmth and human living conditions attracted fleas, and rats were drawn to settlements by the inevitable piles of rubbish. The fatal effect of rats and fleas is well known to those familiar with medieval European history. Whilst we do not have any actual evidence for bubonic plague from pharaonic Egypt – the disease kills so quickly it doesn't have time to leave any physical traces on bones – there are references to 'plagues' in Egypt and other areas of the ancient Near Eastern world. Many diseases may be termed 'plagues'. It is difficult to identify particular plague-like diseases from the scant textual references. It is possible that smallpox, a highly infectious virus, was known to the ancient Egyptians. It has been suggested that the lesions on the face of Ramesses V were caused by smallpox, but this has not been proved. The common occurrence of 'plagues' in Egypt may be indicated by one of the titles of the goddess Sekhmet: Lady of Plague. Certainly by the medieval period Egypt was subject to epidemics of 'plague' due to its prominent position in pilgrimage and trading routes. Unfortunately, medieval authors who mention plagues, such as Ibn Ridwan, are not always clear about the nature of these outbreaks and so a firm identification of the disease (or diseases) is difficult, but it is likely they were frequently a part of Egyptian life. Further evidence of rats was the presence of a pottery rat trap found by Petrie at Kahun and it is thought that the holes stuffed with rubbish found in nearly every Kahun house are indicative of an invasion by these rodents.

As in other developing civilisations, initially only animals which were of some use – providing foodstuffs or traction – were taken into the homestead. Cattle were the most important farm animals on an estate. Various tomb paintings, and in particular, a wooden model of a cattle census from the Eleventh Dynasty tomb of Meketre show the variety of cattle that was bred for meat, milk and dairy products. Goats and pigs, being less particular about their diet, were an economical source of meat. In addition the goat provided milk and skins. The Egyptians had two kinds of sheep – those with short and curled spiral horns and a type with a long spiralled horn – both of which were a possible source of meat and wool; however, certain sections of society were forbidden to eat mutton or wear woollen garments for religious reasons. Despite the valuable contribution animals made to life, they unfortunately brought health problems with them. Many animals were (and are) subject to parasites through which diseases could be transmitted due to the animal's proximity to humans. Cattle spread a form of tuberculosis through infected meat and milk. In addition beef, along with pork, is subject to taenia (tapeworm) infestation and these worms are easily picked up by humans. Sheep and dogs can also relay hydatid disease through this parasite.

There was a limited amount of pastoral and cultivatable land in ancient Egypt and yet a fairly wide range of foodstuffs was grown. Because of underground springs some of the more arid areas, such as the Fayum, developed oases which produced a variety of fruits. The Egyptian farmer had to work fairly hard but the results were rewarding. Research has suggested that agriculture had begun in Egypt by the Predynastic period. Egyptian farmers refined their agricultural techniques by developing a basin irrigation system. Until the water lifting device known as the *shaduf* was introduced during the New Kingdom period, water was moved by this method. The heavy labour of farming and carrying water took its toll on the backs of the labourers (this will be discussed in a later section). The resulting abundance of foodstuffs from these labours eventually freed some of the populace from food-producing duties to allow them to concentrate on developing other skills such as pottery making, building, metal working, administration and so on. All these developments helped lay the foundations for a powerful civilisation but unfortunately this in itself resulted in new health problems. As mentioned before, certain diseases (such as tuberculosis) thrive in crowded living conditions. The larger the population the greater was the likelihood of diseases spreading, though in fact the population figures never seem to have reached a problematic level.

In 1660 George Herbert wrote 'Whosoever was the father of a disease, an ill diet was the mother'. This may be true of many populations but it is unlikely to apply to ancient Egypt for, at a time when many cultures were dependent upon hunting or a few staple foods, the ancient Egyptians were already enjoying a reasonably healthy and for some, a varied diet (plate II). Except in times of famine due to the Nile flooding too little or too much, most members of Egyptian society could expect an adequate diet. Peasant farmers and other everyday workmen and their families consumed a basic diet of bread, beer, fish and vegetables. Bread, the 'staff of life', was the staple part of a meal. The Egyptians enjoyed a wide variety of breads and cakes made from emmer or einkorn wheat or from barley. In the New Kingdom, for example, at least thirty different types of breads and cakes are known to have been produced from the evidence of ancient texts and paintings. Fruits, milk and honey were some of the ingredients added to them to make them more nutritious and appetising. Herodotus (Book II, 91) tells us that Egyptians living in Lower Egypt's marshy areas learned how to live cheaply and economically by making bread from the heads of locally grown lotus plants. It is ironic that the mainstay of the Egyptian diet was also responsible for many of the people's dental problems (see Chapter 7). Vegetables such as onions, leeks, cucumbers, lettuce and garlic and pulses such as lentils and chick-peas were grown by villagers and on the estates of officials. These, together with fruits such as dates, grapes, figs and melons, provided many of the vitamins essential for good health.

Vitamin A is important for skeletal growth and a severe deficiency of it results in the cessation of bone growth in the cranium and spinal areas. This in turn results in the spinal cavity becoming too small for the central nervous system, leading eventually to paralysis. Vitamin A deficiency can also produce eye defects such as night-blindness (nyctalopia) and the more serious xerophthalmia which affects the cornea of the eye. The Ebers Medical Papyrus provides one of the earliest references to an eye problem (probably nyctalopia) and ox liver – rich in vitamin A – is recommended as an effective treatment. Contrasting with this, an excess of vitamin A results in the skeletal growth processes being accelerated and as the epiphyses are prematurely closed linear growth is retarded. Vitamin A is also found in animal fats and oils.

Vitamin B is found in fresh meat and in the outer layers of cereals. A deficiency of this vitamin leads to the condition known as beriberi which affects the heart and the nerves. As the symptoms of this condition are less distinctive than for others associated with vitamin deficiency, it is difficult to detect references to it in early texts.

Vitamin C (ascorbic acid), found in fresh fruit and vegetables, is an important part of the diet and a deficiency of it results in scurvy, a condition in which there is bleeding into the skin and beneath the periosteum. The typical symptoms of scurvy are frequent haemorrhaging and severe ulceration of the gums. Classical authors such as Pliny and Hippocrates observed physical changes typical of scurvy but the condition is unlikely to have occurred widely in ancient Egypt because of the easy access to the necessary fruit and vegetables.

Vitamin D maintains a balance of calcium and phosphorus

enabling the bone matrix to calcify. A deficiency promotes a calcium imbalance which inhibits bone growth and composition. This results in rickets (in children) and osteomalacia (in adults). Weight-bearing bones, especially the femora and tibiae, become bowed and distorted. Vitamin D is obtained from dairy products, fish-liver oils and from exposure to sunlight. As most of the inhabitants of Egypt are likely to have had fish in their diet and adequate sunshine, again it seems unlikely that much evidence for rickets will be seen. It may have been possible that a child (or even an adult) by virtue of the dictates of the family or because of invalid status was discouraged from going outside, and could have developed rickets, but there is no firm evidence for this. Probably the most famous (and controversial) evidence for rickets are the drawings from Amarna and Beni Hasan where the figures appear to have bowed legs. The same individuals, discussed in Chapter 4, also seem to have the congenital condition clubfoot. An excess of vitamin D can cause problems by producing an overload of calcium salts which are then deposited in the soft tissues.

In addition to the vitamins contained in the staple foods and meats mentioned above, protein was provided by poultry and eggs. Geese and ducks are economical to rear and may have been bred by ordinary families. Except on special festival occasions it is unlikely that the poorer families ate meat from the larger animals enjoyed by the wealthier sections of society, but they were at least spared the consequences of eating rich and fatty foods. We have already seen that beef, mutton, goat flesh and poultry were eaten, but the extent to which pork was eaten remains undecided. Herodotus (Book II, 45) relates that pigs were considered unclean and that its flesh was only eaten on the day a pig was sacrificed to two deities. We must remember that Herodotus was writing during the fifth century BC and so was recording events at the end of the pharaonic period. Also we cannot be sure that he observed details correctly or that he was given complete information by the native Egyptians he spoke to. It is even possible that Herodotus may not have actually been to Egypt. From his evidence, it has been thought by some researchers that pork was not eaten in ancient Egypt but the growing archaeological evidence suggests otherwise. That pork was eaten during predynastic times is evident from porcine bones found as household refuse. A scene from the Sixth Dynasty mastaba tomb of Kagemni even shows a man holding a piglet to his mouth to give it food, and this suggests that pigs were certainly valued during the Old Kingdom period. Evidence from excavations at Amarna strongly suggest that the workmen's village attached to the city had an area devoted to the rearing and processing of pigs and their flesh. At times pigs were considered taboo, possibly due to the observation made by many

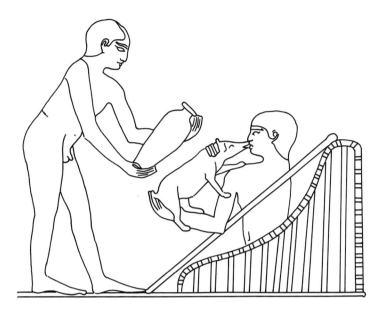

5 *A man holding a piglet to his mouth to feed it. Mastaba of Kagemni, Sixth Dynasty, from Saqqara.*

Middle Eastern societies that pork goes off quickly in warm climates, and that if not cooked thoroughly can harbour tapeworm parasites. Some of the worms found in Nakht, in Toronto, showed that he had eaten inadequately cooked pork.

Wealthier members of society supplemented their diet with more 'exotic' fare. Funerary reliefs show that a plentiful and varied diet was highly valued by the élite. Gazelle and antelope were sometimes eaten and to judge from the many banqueting and butchery scenes large amounts of meat were required. Honey was relished and incorporated into drinks, cakes and breads. As might be expected all this rich living had its consequences for those who over-indulged. Arteriosclerosis (hardening of the arteries due to an over-fatty diet) has been found in mummies as illustrious as the pharaohs Ramesses II and Merenptah. Rich and overly sweetened foods naturally took their toll on the teeth as will be seen in the section on dental health. One very obvious concomitant of indulgence in rich foods and wines can be seen in Egyptian art. At banquets, guests are sometimes seen vomiting, presumably having enjoyed a little too much wine. Gout could be another unpleasant and longer-lasting consequence of excessive wine drinking. However, to judge from the majority of depictions of the well-to-do, one would think that obesity did not exist. Important people are portrayed in the ideal states of youth and slimness, although sometimes men are sometimes shown with stylised rolls of fat, denoting their high status and success in life. Examinations of mummies have revealed the truth – that many ancient Egyptians were overweight.

6 *A woman vomiting, possibly after excessive eating and drinking at a banquet.*

For those wishing to maintain a healthier lifestyle there were a variety of sports to engage in. Wrestling was depicted in several tombs. An excellent portrayal of 'free-style' wrestling is in the tomb of Ptahhotep (Fifth Dynasty) where the tomb owner's son is wrestling with another youth. There are many examples of wrestling in the Middle Kingdom tombs of Beni Hasan: Amenemhet (tomb no. 2), Baqti III (tomb no. 15), Khety (tomb no. 17) and so on. The actions depicted involve exploratory moves and swings and throws, and overall there is an atmosphere of agility and fitness. Stick fighting and boxing were other ways of maintaining strength and fitness and are also depicted in tombs. The élite greatly enjoyed hunting. There are other scenes which seem to show that massage and pedicures were an important part of the fitness and hygiene routine.

When thinking about the effects of the environment on health it is important to consider life expectancy and population density. Karl Butzer has attempted a calculation of the population during various periods of Egyptian history. For the Old Kingdom period a figure of about 1.6 million was suggested. A figure of 2 million has been suggested for the peak of the Middle Kingdom period when Egypt was recovering from the economic decline of previous years. Butzer suggested that by the peak of the New Kingdom period the population had reached a figure of 3 million. A person was open to the greatest risks to health during infancy and early childhood and, as in many ancient populations, there was a high infant mortality rate in ancient Egypt and Nubia. In many cemetery excavations it is not unusual to find that over thirty per cent of the burials are those of children. Some Egyptian and Nubian burial sites, however, yield a low number of youngsters, but this does not necessarily mean that the children were healthy and lived into adulthood. Children's bones do not always survive as well as the more robust adult bones and in some societies children are not always buried in the same places as adults. Their size means they are an attractively portable food for insects,

7 *Skeleton of an infant from Soba, Sudan, sixth to thirteenth centuries AD. In ancient times a high percentage of children died in their first year of life.*

rodents and other scavengers. Furthermore, burial methods and conditions (whether mummified, in a coffin, or placed directly in sand) affect the preservation and survival of the young in various ways, as indeed they do for adults.

Some children's bodies allow us to establish the cause of death, for example tuberculosis or other diseases, but this is rare. In the main a particular cause of death cannot be pinned down but certain clues on the skeleton may indicate the child underwent a period of stress. Cribra orbitalia (where bone tissue in the upper areas of the eye sockets become spongy and vascular) can indicate anaemia through inadequate diet or through illness. G. Armelagos and colleagues recorded many examples of cribra orbitalia in Nubian skeletons. Lines of arrested growth (Harris lines) may be seen, via X-rays, towards the ends of long bones. Harris lines are 'scars' deposited on the metaphyseal parts of the bone shafts as the result of episodes of restricted growth which occur for one reason or another during that individual's lifetime. Under normal circumstances the growth of a

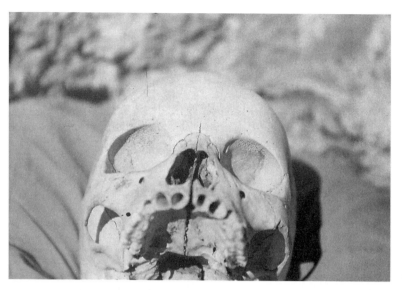

8 *Cribra orbitalia, or pitting in the upper parts of the eye sockets, might be an indicator of periods of illness or dietary problems. An example from Gabati, Sudan.*

long bone, during childhood and adolesence, follows a set pattern. The epiphysis (a detached cap) is separated from each end of the main bone shaft by a band of cartilage. This cartilage deposits new bone on to the main shaft and so elongation occurs. Eventually, after a period of growth, the epiphyses fuse with the main bone shaft preventing any further growth of the bone. If this process of development is interrupted indefinitely by periods of stress followed by recovery, a transverse line of calcification is deposited in the bone. These Harris lines may be used to detect stressful episodes, such as illness, in an individual's life and may be used to compare the health status of various populations. It is also thought that Harris lines can indicate periods of nutritional stress and researchers have noted the resemblance between these transverse lines on human bones and 'hunger bars' seen on the feathers of captive birds.

It is probable that a high number of infants died of illnesses which left no traces on the corpse. It is also likely that the most significant cause of health problems for them were diarrhoeal disorders causing severe loss of water which may have in turn caused loss of kidney function; no evidence of this, however, remains. Diarrhoeal disorders occur for many reasons, including intestinal infection due to dysentery and infection from the typhoid bacillus which may be the result of poor sanitation. Diarrhoeal problems can also be caused by food contaminated by bacteria. The period of weaning, when an infant changes from breast feeding to a more solid diet, is also fraught with high risks as the child is then exposed to new infections.

Texts claim that some individuals lived to a ripe old age, often 110. Sometimes historical longevity is confirmed by the examination of

9 *This burial of a mother and her baby reminds us of the dangers of childbirth in ancient societies. Gabati, Sudan, possibly an early Christian burial.*

the extant body, as in the case of Ramesses II who was at least in his seventies when he died. Examinations of other mummies and skeletons, however, suggest that life expectancy for most Egyptians and Nubians was much shorter. On average men lived some thirty-five years and women about five years less. Women's health (and life expectancy) was considerably weakened by child bearing.

Egyptians engaged in many different types of work, some of which affected their health. In the Twelfth Dynasty text 'Satire of the

Trades' the scribe Khety tries to convince his son that the scribal profession is the best of all. His comparison of scribal activities with other occupations in Egypt emphasises the easier sedentary life of the scribe. About farming the text says 'And the farmer laments more than the guinea fowl, his voice louder than the raven's, with his fingers swollen and excessive stink. He is weary having been assigned to the Delta.' A large percentage of the population were engaged in agricultural activities. The effects of such labours on the spine and joints may have been severe and the probability of picking up parasites from water was high. Associated activities such as carrying heavy loads may also put adverse strain on the back. Various texts describing military expeditions and soldiers' personal letters testify to their harsh life. Records of military expeditions often claimed that an expedition 'returned without any loss' which implies that loss was an expected danger. Apart from the very real dangers of injury through military action (see the chapter on trauma) the soldier might also suffer from exhaustion and lack of food whilst on the march and from bouts of infection. People engaged in building works were subject to bumps and bruises and more serious fractures as the scene of decorating a shrine from the tomb of the architect Ipy intimates. Quarrymen and stone masons, especially those working in the closely confined spaces of tombs were likely to contract silicosis through the inhalation of stone dust. Fishermen and others working on the Nile were in danger of contracting internal parasites and suffering boating accidents. In ancient times there was also a very real danger from crocodiles lurking in the Nile waters. In contrast to these occupations, the life of the scribe and that of the priest was leisurely and free from stress, but high-ranking occupations were not free from the threat of illness, nor, as we have seen, the effects of over-indulgence.

CHAPTER TWO

Sources of Evidence

I n the study of ancient diseases it is very useful to be able to evaluate a variety of sources to give a more rounded picture of a disorder. We are fortunate that Egypt offers a range of biological, written and artistic sources.

BIOLOGICAL SOURCES

Skeletal remains and any extant soft tissues provide the most informative evidence for disease. As will be explained below, written and artistic sources might be subject to the 'bias' of an author or artist who may select which aspects of a disease to describe or depict. Human remains, however, provide irrefutable evidence that a disease process has occurred. It is true that the actual identification of a disease in human remains may provoke debate, even disagreement, but here at least the evidence has not been pre-selected as is possible with other sources. It is important to distinguish between genuine pathological lesions and those which imitate disease. Scavengers, such as rodents and beetles, can attack bone leaving marks which can be confused with pathological features. Similarly, roots of trees and plants can cause striations on bone. Alternating extremes of temperature, moisture and the chemical constituents of soil can also leave marks imitating disease. Once these pseudo-pathologies have been eliminated the work of identifying the disease can begin. Some of the technological methods of investigating disease are outlined in Chapter 3. Soft tissue remains offer another source of detecting disease from the past. Due to the excellently preserved bodies from ancient Egypt and Nubia there are ample opportunities to study both skeletal and soft tissue remains.

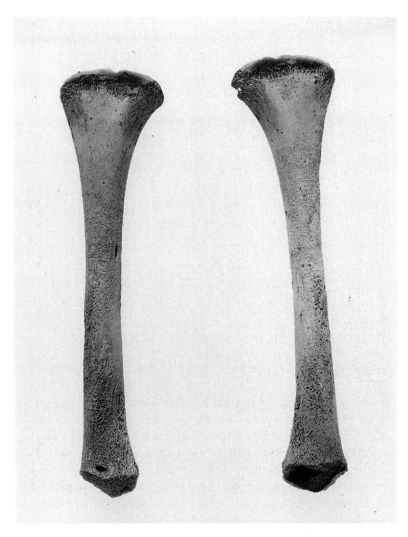

10 *Damage on bones by insects can often imitate pathological lesions. At first sight these limb bones might appear to have a disease, but the true nature of the problem (insect gnawing) was revealed by examination under a high-powered microscope. Infant from Soba, Sudan, sixth to thirteenth centuries AD.*

A powerful influence on the development of Egyptian civilisation was a belief in an existence after death. This was expressed through the provision of funerary gifts and the preservation of the corpse. During the Predynastic period (before 3000 BC) graves were generally shallow pits into which the corpse was introduced. Consequently, the body was in direct contact with the hot desert sands which dessicated the body and prevented further decay. Examples of these sand-dried bodies can be seen in many museums including the British Museum, the Turin Museum and the University Museum of Pennsylvania. Recent excavations at Gabati, Central Sudan, by the Sudan Archaeological Research Society have brought to light many skeletons from the post-Meroitic period with skin, hair (plate III) and brain tissue which are being studied by J.M. Filer. Ironically, later attempts to provide the dead with better grave goods and protection through superstructures, of firstly wood and later of stone, led to the body being separated from the preservative effects of the sand. Initial attempts at artificial mummification consisted merely of wrapping the body in layers of linen bandages. Mummification techniques improved throughout the Dynastic period and into the Graeco-Roman periods reaching a peak of sophistication during the Twenty-first Dynasty (c.1000 BC). The procedure was costly and only available to the relatively wealthy. Throughout this book reference will be made to diseases found in mummies and on skeletons from different periods of Egyptian history, and where possible supporting evidence from written and artistic sources will be given.

ARTISTIC SOURCES

Wall paintings, reliefs, drawings and sculptures can provide supporting information in the study of disease but they should be used with great caution as their representations are determined by cultural factors, such as ideology.

In some instances there can be little doubt as to the condition portrayed but in other cases a careful appraisal of the information is needed. As will be seen in Chapter 4 a particular form of dwarfism (achondroplasia) is well attested from ancient Egypt through extant skeletons. Yet, even without the evidence of the physical remains, artistic representations would tell us that the disorder actually existed in ancient Egypt. Many examples of wall reliefs show the short limbs and stature of dwarfism and the clearest evidence for the condition is found amongst Old Kingdom statuary, now in Cairo Museum, and in a dwarf-figure on a boat-shaped centre piece from the Eighteenth Dynasty tomb of Tutankhamun. In these examples there can be no doubt as to the intention of the craftsmen.

Tuberculosis, as will be seen in Chapter 5, has a long attested history in Egypt and Nubia, the evidence emanating from both physical remains and from works of art. Yet some of the artistic examples need to be more closely examined and evaluated. Certain clay figures depicting men, which may date to the Predynastic period, have long been thought to represent cases of tuberculosis. The humped spine and the noticeably emaciated look of the figures make a diagnosis of Pott's disease (that is, tuberculosis of the spine) extremely plausible. Yet the fact that some of these figures sit in large pottery vessels might suggest the alternative interpretation that they are reflecting a style of burial. In the Petrie Museum, University College, London, for example, an adult skeleton from the predynastic site of Hemamieh, sits in a contracted position in a large red-ware

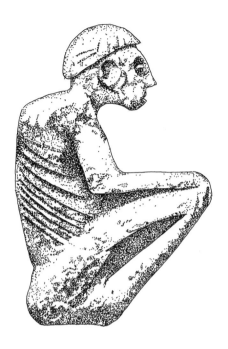

11 *One of the predynastic clay figures, often found in pots, which could be subject to various interpretations, including a depiction of spinal tuberculosis.*

pot. Whilst representation of tuberculosis of the spine may be the probable intent of the artist, is it not a possible alternative that the clay figure in a pot is an artistic representation of this early type of burial? From this example it becomes obvious that some pieces of art may be subject to more than one interpretation.

The figure of a gardener shown in the tomb of Ipwy (Nineteenth Dynasty) lifting a *shaduf*, also appears to have the humped back denoting Pott's disease. It might be supposed that this is a badly drawn shoulder for it is well known that on occasion ancient Egyptian artists depicted shoulder joints in certain postures as if 'folded in', which can give the impression of a hunched spine. Ipwy's gardener, viewed in isolation, might be a candidate for such an interpretation except that his is not the only figure shown in this gardening scene. He is flanked, on both sides, by other men engaged in the same occupation, each leaning forward to manoeuvre a *shaduf*. Even a cursory glance at these figures reveals the other men to have normally set shoulder joints and spines. Thus, a comparison between the distorted figure and his fellow workers indicates that a depiction of symptoms suggestive of spinal tuberculosis was intended.

A figure with very clear physical symptoms can none the less be open to various interpretations concerning possible identification of the disease; one example is that of the Queen of Punt. A relief on a wall of the Temple of Hatshepsut at Deir el-Bahri from the Eighteenth Dynasty shows the Punt Queen, her husband and two children receiving an Egyptian royal emissary prior to trading negotiations. The Queen of Punt has an abnormally curved lower spine and is excessively obese with rolls of fat hanging from her arms and legs. The Queen's condition has been variously attributed to bilateral hip deformity, steatopygia and Dercum's disease. Several researchers have suggested that the Queen suffered from a congenitally determined dysplasia (or abnormal growth) of the hip joints which led to dislocation. As hip dysplasias frequently occur in related individuals it would be interesting to know if her daughter had inherited the same condition. Unfortunately, the figure of the Queen's daughter, also depicted in the relief, is now difficult to see clearly. Elliot Smith and Wood Jones described the bodies of five women from the Christian colony near the Temple of Philae with hip-joint dysplasia who were likely to have been related. Certainly in the Queen of Punt relief the daughter appears fairly obese but a diagnosis of congenital hip dysplasia must remain hypothetical. Steatopygia, or excessive development of fat on the buttocks is not, in itself, an abnormal or diseased condition but is in fact a racial characteristic as seen in modern Hottentot groups. But as the mysterious land of Punt was more likely to have been in East rather than South Africa where the Hottentots or Bushmen originate true steatopygia is an unlikely cause of the Queen of Punt's obesity. This leaves us with lipodystrophy, or Dercum's disease which is characterised by curvature of the spine, fatty deposits on the buttocks and large accumulations of subcutaneous fat on the arms and legs which can be quite painful as nerve lesions are often involved. An examination of the Hatshepsut relief would seem to support the idea of Dercum's disease. It has also been suggested that the queen was simply, and unpathologically, overweight and that possibly Egyptian craftsmen, in trying to depict reported stories of a foreign queen who they had never seen themselves, exaggerated her obesity. Certainly, the queen's obese figure contrasts sharply with the Egyptian idea of feminine beauty where women are depicted as slim. However, the fact that the queen presents a tight chin line with no facial rolls of fat together with the rather pronounced curvature of the lower spine are more suggestive of a pathological condition.

'To no other time in Egyptian history has reconstruction been so lavishly applied by ingenious minds.' Thus wrote W. Stevenson Smith about the Amarna period (1372–1350 BC), a period which more than any other in Egyptian history illustrates the need to view works of art within their historical context without hailing them unreservedly as examples of ancient pathology. The art of the Amarna period is dominated by the figure of the king Akhenaten (who changed his name from Amenophis IV), his chief wife Nefertiti

and their daughters. A striking feature of the art of this period is the different way in which the human form is represented particularly with regard to the proportions of the body.

The words of W. Stevenson Smith could easily apply to medical historians and palaeopathologists themselves who for so long have tried ingeniously to construct a medical diagnosis based upon the many representations of Akhenaten, both in relief and statuary, which show the king with unusual physical features. A colossal statue and a head, originally from Karnak and now in the Cairo Museum, for example, show Akhenaten with an elongated face and upward slanting eyes, a pendulous jaw and full lips. The body of the statue shows the king with the feminine attributes of wide hips, breast and full thighs which have encouraged researchers to suggest a variety of possible causes, from hermaphroditism (having physical attributes of both sexes) to Fröhlich's Syndrome. In this latter condition males exhibit a feminine type of bodily fat distribution on the thighs, buttocks, breast and abdomen. A common cause of Fröhlich's Syndrome is a tumour of the pituitary gland which affects fat distribution

12 *Pott's disease: the right-hand central figure in this gardening scene from the tomb of Ipwy appears to have spinal tuberculosis. Nineteenth Dynasty.*

within the body and may also promote excessive growth of the jaw. However, an important concomitant to Fröhlich's Syndrome is the sufferer's inability to father children. Since the famous Nefertiti is known to have given birth to six daughters and she was the wife of Akhenaten several scenarios present themselves. If the king did have Fröhlich's Syndrome then the Amarna princesses must have been fathered by another person, with Akhenaten publicly acknowledging them as his own children. Alternatively, if Akhenaten was the natural father of the girls, as sources state, he could not have suffered from this condition. If the latter is the case, then another reason must be sought to explain the unusual artistic representations of the king's physique. The unusual features may be artistic convention rather than a record of anatomical oddities. Indeed it is important to note that representations of the king during the earlier part of his reign show him with quite normal features and in one depiction he was shown unshaven; males suffering from Fröhlich's Syndrome, however, do not grow facial hair. Furthermore, other high-ranking court officials of this period were depicted in a similar manner, one of

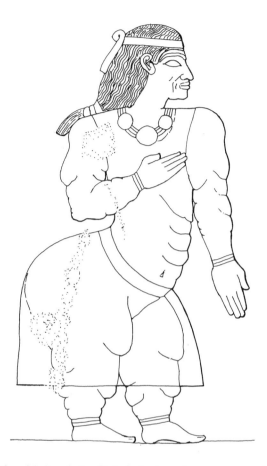

13 *The Queen of Punt.
The curvature of her spine
and excessive amounts of
fat may indicate a
pathological condition.
Temple of Hatshepsut,
Eighteenth Dynasty.*

note being the chief sculptor Bak (who has the pronounced abdomen
often seen in the Amarna period) and his wife. Are we to suppose that
many court officials suffered from a similar complaint to that of the
king, or that they were depicted in the new style in flattering
imitation of the king's deformities? The answer may lie instead in
Akhenaten's own philosophy and artistic reforms. Since the early
Eighteenth Dynasty there had been a growing regard for and worship
of the Aten sun-disc as a manifestation of the sun-god but it was
Akhenaten who broke with traditional religious values, and denied
the reality of the many Egyptian gods in favour of one god, the Aten.

In a short hymn to the Aten, versions of which are found in five
Amarna period tombs, the sun-disc is addressed as 'mother and
father of all that you made' and this sentiment may be at the heart of
Akhenaten's religious philosophy. The Aten, as a disc, is neither male
nor female but the creator of both. The king, as the earthly representation of the Aten might thus have been depicted as both male and
female; Akhenaten is shown with characteristics of both sexes to

14 *A statue of Akhenaten, now in the Cairo Museum, showing the king with a feminine distribution of fat on the breasts, thighs and buttocks.*

show that he is the mother and father of his people. In this view Akhenaten is not suffering from a pathological condition but is outwardly expressing his religious doctrine through art.

It has also been suggested that Akhenaten and his daughters suffered from some degree of hydrocephalus, a condition discussed in Chapter 4. Again, the 'evidence' is supplied by works of art and is not backed up by any anatomical evidence. It is true that several depictions of the family show exceptionally elongated skulls, such as in the wall painting of the Amarna princesses in the Ashmolean Museum, Oxford, but in the absence of any skeletal remains these cannot be judged as representing reality. The same condition is shown in other (non-royal) people of the period. Another family member, the young king Tutankhamun, was also judged to be hydrocephalic yet upon anatomical investigation it was seen that his skull measurements fell within the normal range. Some controversial remains from Tomb 55 in the Valley of the Kings have at various times been attributed to Akhenaten or Smenkhare (a king who ruled briefly after Akhenaten), but without any certainty. Here the skull from Tomb 55 appears overly long but again falls within normal anatomical limits. The truth of the matter is, that in the absence of identifiable human remains, the whole question of the physical appearance of Akhenaten must remain an enigma. The question of the Amarna royal family and artificially shaped heads will be discussed in Chapter 6 in relation to trauma.

The skeleton of the dwarf Perenankh (Fifth or Sixth Dynasty) was found by Z. Hawass at Giza with his funerary statue. This has provided Professor F. Hussein in Cairo with the excellent opportunity of comparing the measurements of both. She has found that the measurements of the foreshortened arms and legs of the skeleton seem to match those of the statue and it may well be that there was a realistic attempt to model Perenankh's skeletal disorder.

In this brief discussion of the value of works of art in identifying disease it can be seen that whilst many representations are unequivocal others must be viewed with caution.

WRITTEN SOURCES

Written sources are useful but again they must be used with caution. Whilst they may record the contemporary impressions of a disease, modern readers may not always recognise that disease. Symptoms which modern medical practitioners would view as crucial to the identification of a disease may not have been considered important in ancient times and so were not recorded.

The medical literature of ancient populations may sometimes reveal how a society viewed sickness and disease and in some cases we are afforded an insight into available treatment. It is likely that the ancient Egyptian medical practitioners had access to a large variety of 'books' for consultation but only a small number of these have survived. To the modern reader the content of some texts seems to have a more magical than medical intent, whilst others appear to have a more practical value. To the ancient medical practitioner, however, these two distinctions were unlikely to be recognised for the spoken word was deemed as valuable as any practical help.

The longest and most complete of the medical texts is the Ebers Papyrus in Leipzig University named after Georg Ebers, the German Egyptologist, who acquired it in the nineteenth century. The document was probably written at the beginning of the Eighteenth Dynasty but is likely to have been copied from a series of older 'books'. The text contains a miscellany of jottings and recipes or prescriptions for numerous ailments including eye and skin diseases, stomach complaints, boils and cysts, coughs, bites, women's diseases and so on. One section relates to the actions of the heart and veins whilst others suggest remedies for ridding the house of vermin or suggest ways of improving personal appearance. The prescriptions specify the drugs (herbs, plants, even urine and excreta) to be used and their method of preparation and application.

Attempts were made to translate the text, notably by H. Joachim in 1890 and by B. Ebbell in 1937, but neither of these can be regarded as satisfactory. Translation from ancient texts is always fraught with the difficulty of trying to translate a language, such as ancient Egyptian, which is no longer used. Frequently, especially in medical texts, it is impossible to identify the ancient Egyptian word for a known disease or ingredient (such as a herb or plant) particularly when it is not described. For the ancient Egyptian reader of such texts detailed description of such things was unnecessary as they were familiar items.

The Edwin Smith Papyrus, acquired by its owner in 1862, probably had a Theban origin like the Ebers. The two papyri may even have originally been found together. The text dates from the New Kingdom but, again, is likely to be a copy of a much older document, since the text contains glosses (or marginal notes) explaining 'old-fashioned' vocabulary to the more 'modern' reader of New Kingdom Egypt. The Edwin Smith Papyrus was translated by J. H. Breasted in 1930. The Edwin Smith Papyrus is often termed the Surgical Papyrus because it describes different types of injuries and how to treat them. The text, which contains forty-eight surgical cases, obviously intended to deal with injury to all parts of the body in topographical order from the head downwards. However, after describing cases of injury to the thorax, the author (or scribe) stops in mid-sentence in the first case of treatment for spinal injury. The text is arranged systematically under the following categories: a description of the injury; instructions for examining the patient and for eliciting information; a diagnosis and a prognosis giving one of three possible outcomes – success, possible success or untreatable. Where deemed relevant a suitable treatment is suggested. Of particular interest in the Edwin Smith Papyrus are the descriptions and treatment of cranial and facial injuries, some of which are similar to those described in Chapter 6.

The oldest medical texts thus far discovered date to the Middle Kingdom. The Kahun Papyrus which was found in the Fayum area of Egypt in 1889 contains thirty-four sections relating to gynaecological problems and giving methods for controlling fertility and for ascertaining the sex of an unborn child. The Ramesseum Papyri were discovered in 1896 by J. E. Quibell: Papyrus IV deals with similar problems to those of the Kahun Papyrus, whilst V deals with stiffened (possibly arthritic) limbs. Chester-Beatty Papyrus VI, now in the British Museum, dates to the New Kingdom and has been called a fragmentary treatise on proctology as it deals with diseases of the anus and rectum. Other papyri of medical interest are: a Middle Kingdom papyrus in Turin which deals with snake bites and eye

15 *This section from the medical text Chester-Beatty Papyrus VI deals with anal disorders and suggests prescriptions and their application.*

diseases; the London Medical Papyrus (Eighteenth Dynasty) which contains recipes and prescriptions; the Berlin Medical Papyrus (Nineteeth Dynasty) and the Hearst Papyrus (Eighteenth Dynasty) both with contents similar to the Ebers Papyrus, and the Carlsberg Papyrus No. VIII which deals with eye diseases and obstetrics.

The ancient Egyptians always enjoyed a great reputation for their skills in medicine. This is shown in texts from outside Egypt, especially those from the classical world. In Homer's *Odyssey* it is said that the doctors of Egypt were more skilled than those of all other lands. The Egyptians may have had specialists for every part of the body, since Herodotus, writing during the fifth century BC, suggests that doctors specialised in particular areas of the body. The earliest Egyptian with a medical title (Hesy-Re) dates to the Third Dynasty (*c*.2620 BC). His title suggests he specialised in dental problems. Herodotus also relates that King Cyrus sent to Egypt for an eye doctor, and that King Darius was of the opinion that the Egyptians had the highest reputations for their medical practices.

CHAPTER THREE

Modern
Technology and
Ancient Diseases

AUTOPSIES

A nineteenth-century painting by P. Phillipoteaux depicts a group of men standing around a mummy lying on a table (plate IV). The mummy is that of Tawedjatra, an Egyptian priestess, and the gentlemen are French Egyptologists and other interested scholars. Before the advent of modern technology the only way to examine the contents of a mummy was by unwrapping it and performing an autopsy. As can be seen in the painting, it was a destructive and irreversible technique. During the nineteenth century it was not unusual for human and animal mummies to be brought back to Europe as souvenirs by travellers to Egypt. Human mummies were often unrolled as part of a social event, and as can be seen in the painting of the autopsy of Tawedjatra even the more formal investigations of the day were attended by fashionable society ladies. More often than not neither the information observed at these unwrappings nor the body itself was retained. We are lucky, however, that at least some investigators undertook to examine mummies in a more rigorous manner and publish their findings.

In 1825, Augustus Granville, a physician to the Duke of Cumberland, published an account of his examination of an Egyptian mummy. The mummy, which is that of a woman named Irtyersenu, is probably from the Twenty-sixth Dynasty or later, to judge by the style of coffin lid which accompanies the body. The coffin (of which only the lid survives) and its contents were given to Granville in 1821 by Sir Archibald Edmonstone who had originally paid about four dollars for them. Granville in his own words decided to 'sacrifice a most complete specimen of the Egyptian art of embalming in hopes of eliciting some new facts illustrative of so curious and interesting a subject'. He judged the lady to have been between fifty and fifty-five years of age at death and that she had borne children. Two issues were of palaeopathological interest. The lady had porrigo decalvans, a cutaneous affection of the head which destroys the hair as well as preventing its growth. During the autopsy Granville noted the lady's uterus had been diseased for some time prior to death. In his publication of 1825 Granville was of the opinion that 'the disease which appears to have destroyed her was ovarian dropsy'. That she had some ovarian disease was indeed correct but the diagnosis of dropsy (or cancer) has recently been refuted and is discussed in Chapter 5. An examination of the mummy's lung tissue has revealed pneumonia, and this is the most likely cause of the lady's death.

Another nineteenth-century unwrapping and dissection resulted in an address being made to the Leeds Literary and Philosophical Society by William Osburn in 1828. The subject of the address was the mummy of a middle-aged priest named Nesamun who had lived during the Twentieth Dynasty. As this mummy had been unwrapped there was little reason why it could not be examined again in 1989 and so the team responsible for studying the Manchester mummies re-appraised the mummy of Nesamun. Although the dead man's name is now read as Nesamun, the investigating team decided to retain the reading Natsef-Amun, as in the original publication of 1828. As might have been expected the priest had badly worn teeth, a

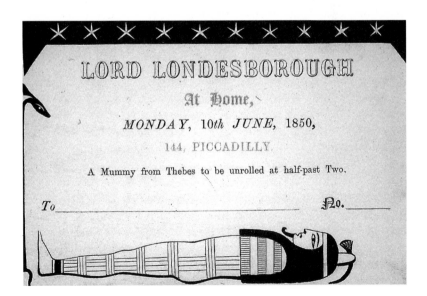

16 *An invitation to the unwrapping of an Egyptian mummy.*

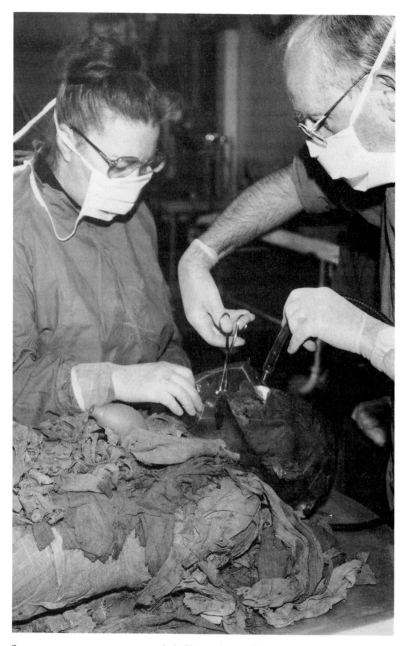

17 *A.R. David and E. Tapp taking samples for testing during the Manchester Mummy team's examination of the Leeds mummy.*

feature common to many adult Egyptians. Osteoarthritis had started in his left hip and changes in his cervical spine suggest that during life he suffered intermittent pains in his neck. Like many ancient Egyptians, Nesamun had a worm infestation and it is possible he had an eye condition called peripheral neuritis, caused by the degeneration of nerve fibres.

Another nineteenth-century medical man, Thomas Pettigrew, was also interested in Egyptian mummies and their diseases. Fortunately he too recorded his findings and in 1834 he published what was then a comprehensive account of the embalming of human and animal corpses. In many ways Pettigrew's working procedure was the forerunner of modern mummy research in that experts from a variety of fields were consulted in a multi-disciplinary approach. Pettigrew unrolled and autopsied many mummies before audiences of medical and scientific personnel together with the usual complement of the leading socialites of the day.

Another early, but informative, investigation of a mummy was undertaken by Dr Margaret Murray in Manchester in 1908. Two mummies known as the Two Brothers – Khnumnakht and Nakhtankh – had been found with their funerary goods in their undisturbed tomb at Rifeh in Middle Egypt. A careful study of the two men suggested that they were, in fact, half-brothers sharing the same mother. Physical characteristics of the younger brother Khnumnakht suggested that his father was from a different ethnic group. Khnumnakht suffered from osteoarthritis in his back and the unusual shape of his left foot is discussed in the chapter on congenital diseases. In the 1970's Richard Neave, a medical artist, made head and facial reconstructions from the two men's skulls, and as two carved wooden statuettes purportedly of the two brothers were part of the funerary goods, these reconstructions could be compared with the statuettes. Each statuette compared favourably with its reconstruction and the physical differences between the two men can be clearly seen.

At the beginning of this century some six thousand bodies from Nubian cemeteries were retrieved before the rising Nile waters caused by the filling of the new Aswan Dam could submerge them. The bodies, from most periods of Nubian history, were examined by Grafton Elliot Smith an anatomist living in Cairo. He was assisted firstly by Dr F. Wood Jones and then by Dr D. E. Derry. From these bodies a fairly comprehensive picture of burial practices and the incidence of various diseases was built up. Elliot Smith was later able to continue his research into the history and techniques of mummification when he had an opportunity to examine the New Kingdom royal mummies. The mummy of Thutmosis IV, a pharaoh of the Eighteenth Dynasty, was publicly unwrapped and examined, and was the first royal mummy to be X-rayed.

The unwrapping and autopsy of an Egyptian mummy named PUM II was carried out in 1973 by A. Cockburn and colleagues as part of a symposium on death and disease in ancient Egypt. The mummy belongs to the Philadelphia Art Museum. The dissection revealed information about mummification techniques and showed that PUM II had inhaled sand during dust storms and suffered from temporal bone disease.

Nearly seventy years after Margaret Murray had examined the mummies of the Two Brothers another historic investigation took place at Manchester. In June 1975 a team of experts led by Dr A. Rosalie David gathered to unwrap a mummy known only as No. 1770. Whilst many Egyptologists feel that it may be unnecessary to unwrap any more mummies because their numbers are limited, it was decided to unwrap this one because its disarrayed outer wrappings made it unsuitable for display. Its provenance was unknown. Mummy No. 1770 had been X-rayed some years before and the resulting radiographs raised enough questions to warrant the new investigation. There was a puzzling absence of soft tissue; the examination revealed that No. 1770, an adolescent girl, had been re-wrapped during the Roman period of Egyptian history which accounts for this anomaly. The mummy also had gold nipple covers (as if it were a female) and an artificial phallus as if it were a male which suggests perhaps that the embalmers of the Roman period were unsure of the sex of the body they were dealing with.

The last time an Egyptian mummy was newly unwrapped and examined in Britain was at Bristol in 1981. The decision to do this was taken because the mummy in question was suffering severe conservation problems. This was an important event because unlike many mummies which are unwrapped and dissected this was the mummy of a named and known individual. Texts on his coffin name him as Horemkenesi, and graffiti in the Theban necropolis have revealed that Horemkenesi was a priest and also chief of workmen in the community of tomb-builders at Deir el-Medina at the end of the New Kingdom. This is a well-documented community, and we know much more about the world Horemkenesi lived in than any other ancient Egyptian community so far studied. Unfortunately much soft tissue information was unavailable as the mummy's internal organs, including the heart, had not been replaced in the body during the mummification process. The embalmers had also failed to remove the brain as was usual in the preparation of the body.

The mummy's poor state of preservation may have been due to Horemkenesi having died far away from proper embalming facilities so that some putrefaction had set in before the body could be treated. The examination of the body revealed that Horemkenesi was middle-aged at death and had suffered from some of the usual ailments, namely worn teeth and osteoarthritis, particularly in his neck which caused stiffness. He also had dental abscesses which must have caused him much discomfort.

18 *Members of the Bristol Mummy team removing linen bandages during the examination of Horemkenesi in 1981.*

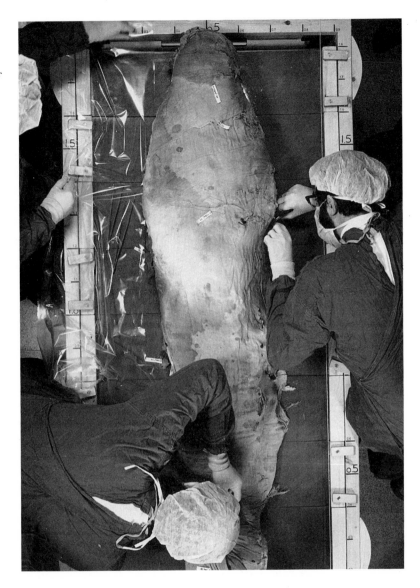

X-RAYS

A rigid mummy travelling in a horse-drawn cab through the busy streets of Cairo must have been a surprise to those who saw the episode. The year was 1904 and Grafton Elliot Smith anatomist was taking the Pharaoh Thutmosis IV to be X-rayed. X-raying was a new procedure and the equipment was both expensive and cumbersome and so, at first, not many mummies were examined through radiography.

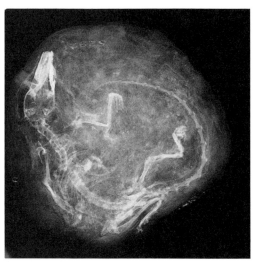

X-rays had been discovered in 1895 by the German physicist Wilhelm Roentgen and one of the first people to realise the potential use of radiography for mummy studies was W. M. F. Petrie. In 1898 Petrie, 'the father of British Egyptology', had examined radiologically a human mummy. He recognised that the main advantage of X-raying over other methods of study was its non-destructive nature. However, it was not until 1931 that a large scale X-ray project examining mummies was attempted, when a collection of Egyptian and Peruvian mummies in Chicago were studied in detail by R. L. Moodie.

Since the pioneering work of Moodie a growing number of biological studies have incorporated radiography in their methodology. During the 1960s Dr P. Gray, a radiographer, X-rayed collections of mummies in Leiden's Rijksmuseum and in the City of Liverpool museums. In 1968, together with Warren Dawson, Gray X-rayed and published a catalogue of the Egyptian mummies and some of the human remains in the British Museum. Those remains which were not included in this catalogue are being examined and catalogued by J. M. Filer. In 1965, a group of American dentists, after studying the dentition of ancient and modern Nubians, were invited to X-ray the mummies of the pharaohs of Egypt in the Cairo Museum. Harris and Wente's study provided information about the dental health of the royal families of ancient Egypt, and was also invaluable in revealing the age at death of the mummies, and indicating some of the types of diseases they suffered from. They proved that despite their higher standard of living, even royalty succumbed to ill health. The X-rays also raised controversial questions about familial relationships amongst some of the royal mummies.

19 and 20 A mummified bundle, the contents of which were unknown. X-ray examination revealed the contents to be a shrew-mouse.

X-rays, like photography, have the problem of depicting a three-dimensional object on a two-dimensional (or flat) plane. Another difficulty is that the rays record everything in their path, so that images often appear to be superimposed one upon another; in practice, however, this presents few problems in interpretation for the experienced radiographer and there can be no doubt about the immense diagnostic value of X-rays. X-rays have revealed, for example, that the contents of a 'mummy' are not always correctly indicated by its external appearance. A small mummy in the British Museum looks like a child, yet an X-ray of the contents show the remains of a bird. Another British Museum 'child' mummy contains only bundles of linen. Other museums also possess similar 'fake' mummies, whose true nature can be revealed by X-rays. During the nineteenth century many European travellers explored Egypt and it was fashionable to bring back a mummy, either human or animal, as a souvenir and, as explained in the previous section, many of these were unrolled and autopsied. The increasing demand for mummies led to the manufacture of fake mummies for the tourist market.

Even when a mummy does contain a human body it is useful to know, through X-rays, how much of a corpse has been preserved. For a variety of reasons the entire body may not be present. The corpse could have started decaying before embalming could take place and so limbs may have been lost. Sometimes embalmers were haphazard in their methods and treated the corpse carelessly, as often occurred during the Roman period when some mummies are disordered inside their wrappings. It is also important to know the gender of an individual. A mummy may be found in a coffin to which it may not have originally belonged. A male mummy may have been put in a coffin made and inscribed for a female, and vice versa, and, as in the case of the Manchester mummy No. 1770, the sex of the corpse may have been unknown. An Egyptian mummy of Roman date in the British Museum has the external appearance of a female with the bandages padded to form breasts. X-rays revealed the mummy's true gender as male. By studying particular features seen on an X-ray, the sex of the mummy can be established. Also certain features will determine its age at death, with a reasonable degree of certainty.

Radiography can also help in understanding embalming (or mummification) techniques. Various methods are known to have been used at particular periods of history and these can be useful in dating the body. X-ray examination will also show if amulets were put in a mummy's wrappings. As amulets (of metal or faience) are radiopaque, their position on the body will show up on the X-ray film.

Radiography is particularly important in palaeopathology, the study of ancient diseases, since both bony lesions and soft tissue lesions can be examined with the help of X-rays. In some cases there may be external evidence of a disease (i.e. a lesion) on a bone but the underlying nature of the condition may need to be clarified. The full extent of the lesion can be examined through X-rays to see if it is localised or if other areas are involved. In this way fractures, osteo-arthritis, dental problems and other conditions can be investigated. X-rays will reveal features that are not a pathological condition in themselves, but which can indicate the prior occurrence of a problem. A case in point might be lines of arrested growth – lines of opacity near the ends of bones – which indicate that the individual had suffered a period of stress, maybe illness or malnutrition, during his or her life. These Harris lines (see fig. 41) show up opaquely on an X-ray enabling a researcher to build up a clearer picture of that person's health history. X-rays of the mummy of a little girl of the Ptolemaic period showed Harris lines in her leg bones. During her life she had suffered from tuberculosis. In the case of mummified bodies extra palaeopathological information can be gained from the soft tissues. Here X-rays can reveal incidences of, for example, ar-teriosclerosis (hardening of the arteries), gallstones and other soft tissue conditions.

XERORADIOGRAPHY

Xeroradiography is a special type of X-ray which uses a high definition technique. In xeroradiography the edges of the resulting images are strongly delineated, which makes shapes easier to see. In 1974, the mummy of Pharaoh Ramesses II was taken to Paris for treatment for a fungal infection, and this gave an opportunity for a detailed examination. Through xeroradiography it was discovered that the pharaoh's nose had been packed by the embalmers with seeds and a small animal bone to make it withstand the pressure of the bandages applied during mummification (plate V).

CT SCANNING

In more recent years another advanced radiographic technique has become available for examining both living and mummified bodies. This technique is called computed tomography (CT) scanning. In this procedure the X-ray film and the source of the rays are moved synchronously and equally in opposing directions to record the body in detail. CT scans have all the advantages of conventional X-rays, but do not suffer from the problem of superimposed images men-tioned earlier. More importantly, the scanner can record images through the body in 'slices' of varying thickness depending upon the area under examination. These 'slices' can be put together to

21 *The mummy of Tjentmutengebtiu, daughter of a priest, entering a CT scanner.*

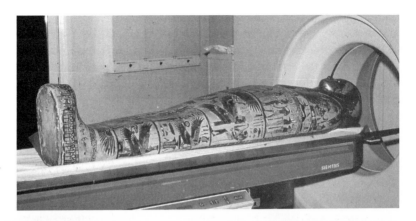

22 *Images of a body can be taken in 'slices' and put together to make a three-dimensional picture as in this mummy, from the Roman period.*

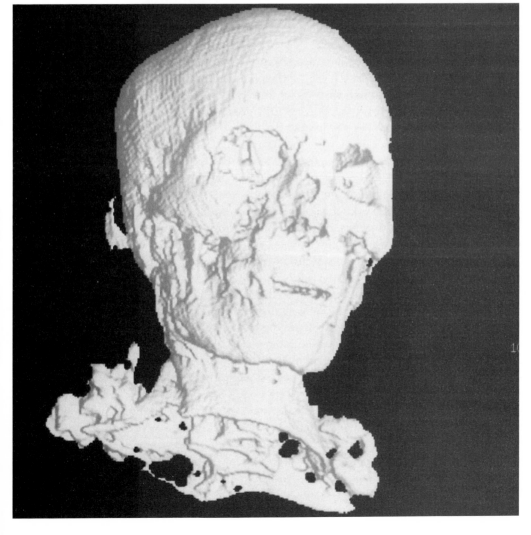

produce a three-dimensional picture of the body. If required, images of particular parts of the body can be isolated and viewed from various angles to give clearer information. The technique is valuable for the study of mummies because it is non-destructive, and through this method of extracting and isolating particular areas of the body pathology can be detected and biological queries about sex and age at death can be answered.

During 1993 the mummy of a Twenty-second Dynasty priestess from the British Museum visited St Thomas's Hospital in London to be CT scanned. CT scans of Tjentmutengebtiu have told us much about her life and state of health, as well as about the mummification techniques used on her body. Tjentmutengebtiu's mummy was of particular interest because the Twenty-second Dynasty was a time of change not only in the decoration of coffins but also in embalming methods. Because it would be destructive to open the sealed carton-nage case CT scanning provided the best method of examination. The resulting scans showed some of the expected aspects of mummi-fication: that the brain had been removed through the nose, that the skull cavity had been stuffed with linen and that amulets with protective powers had been placed at various points on the body. Tjentmutengebtiu's heart was still in place but had shrunk by about 44 per cent and the parcels containing her viscera had been placed not in the abdomen but in the chest. The abdomen itself had actually been filled with packing material. The CT scans were able to help settle the question of the lady's age at death. As a result of Dawson and Gray's X-ray examination of her mummy in 1968 her age had been put at between 25 and 40 years. The developmental stage of her third molar teeth and the amount of wear on all her molars as revealed by the CT scans now suggest that her age at death was between 19 and 23 years.

Like conventional X-rays, computed tomography is a valuable tool for detecting disease in mummies. This can be achieved by varying the depths of field to assess a particular situation. It has been tentatively suggested that Tjentmutengebtiu suffered from Schmorl's nodes, where herniation on the articular surfaces of the vertebral bodies is caused by pressure from the intervertebral discs, which may have been caused by the lifting of heavy objects. CT scanning was first used in palaeopathological investigations in 1974 to study the mummy of Nakht, a temple weaver, in Toronto. CT scans were able to ascertain that it was unnecessary to undertake a destructive examination of Nakht's intact brain as there was no evidence of its being diseased.

In recent years a more refined version of CT scanning, Spiral CT scanning, has been developed. As the name implies, the body is monitored spirally to allow for maximum examination of internal structures.

SCANNING ELECTRON MICROSCOPE

The scanning electron microscope (SEM) has been generally available since 1965, and it is invaluable in revealing and displaying the detailed surface structure of objects. In mummy studies this technique is particularly useful for examining the external 'hard' parts such as teeth, skin, nails and hair. Once the characteristic form of these tissues is established and no further developmental changes occur, they die. This is contrary to the internal 'hard' structures which are living tissues and are subject to continual change and modification. In the examination of the half-brothers Nakhtankh and Khnumnakht at Manchester Museum, for example, the SEM was used to establish the characteristics of their hair and to examine their skin.

ENDOSCOPY

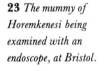
23 *The mummy of Horemkenesi being examined with an endoscope, at Bristol.*

Endoscopy is a technique whereby a narrow tube is inserted into an object via a small hole or incision. The technique is used in modern medical practice as an investigatory procedure prior to surgery. Originally the technique was developed for industrial purposes and

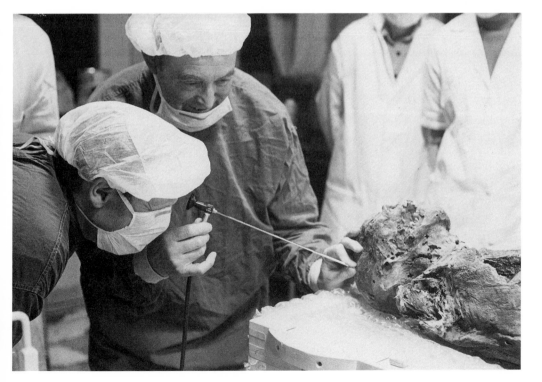

was used for examining inaccessible parts of machines, such as aeroplane wings, for fractures and so on. Endoscopy has also proved useful during the investigation of Egyptian mummies. The endo-scope allows a visual examination of an organ and with the aid of pincers introduced through the tube, a sample of the organ can be obtained and examined histologically. This technique was performed on the head of a mummy in the Manchester Museum (No. 22940) with interesting results. A hydatid cyst was shown in the remaining brain tissue. This infection occurs when a human consumes food infected with the dog tape worm. The cysts, which can form in the lungs, kidneys and liver, can grow up to 5 cm in diameter, but may not always produce symptoms. In the brain, however, the cysts are dangerous, building up pressure to cause headaches and impaired vision and eventually death.

OTHER TECHNIQUES

Other techniques used in biological studies include the exploitation of mitochondrial DNA which is proving informative for Egyptian population studies. Here DNA sequences for modern populations in the Nile Valley are being generated and these will be compared with sequences obtained from ancient human beings, allowing us to map the geographic and cultural demography of the area. This work has already begun in the British Museum where samples from pre-dynastic Egyptian and medieval Nubian bodies are being utilised. DNA studies are moving towards kinship research, sex identification and the identification of diseases.

CHAPTER FOUR

Congenital Disorders

DWARFISM

The statue of Seneb and his family is a good starting point for discussing congenital abnormality in Egypt. Seneb was an important court official during the Sixth Dynasty. It is clear from his shortened arms and legs that Seneb was a dwarf, but in his funerary statue the sculptor cleverly placed his two children in front of their father where his legs would normally have been. This placement not only makes good artistic sense in giving the composition with his seated wife balance but maintains the status and dignity of the man. It is one of the many surviving artefacts which show that dwarfs not only survived to adulthood in ancient Egypt but could enjoy normal life.

Some congenital abnormalities may be inherited genetically or they may be caused by factors adversely affecting the foetus during pregnancy. Sometimes the abnormality may be obvious immediately after birth or the symptoms may present themselves some time after birth during the infant's growing period. Seneb suffered from the form of dwarfism known as achondroplasia which is easily distinguishable in skeletal remains and, although a rare condition, has been portrayed in Egyptian art more often than any other congenital deformity. This condition may be inherited or may occur sporadically as the result of a gene mutation inhibiting the growth of cartilage. The fastest-growing bones of the body are the most severely affected and so the femur and humerus are most noticeably squat and shortened; the forearms and lower leg limbs are also affected. The skull is relatively large with a bulging forehead and in many cases the nasal bridge is depressed. Sometimes there may be some curvature of the spine. The beautifully sculpted dwarf steerswoman on the calcite boat-shaped 'centre-piece' from the tomb of Tutankhamun shows that the Egyptians were aware that the condition affected women as well as men. Warren Dawson has suggested that more males than females were affected in ancient Egypt but this is not certain; in modern times the condition affects both sexes equally. Egyptian art generally depicts more men than women. The short stature of the achondroplastic dwarf should not be confused with that of ethnic pygmies (also in evidence in ancient Egypt) nor with the form of dwarfism associated with endocrine disturbances where the thyroid gland is upset by a severe iodine deficiency resulting in cretinism – a condition presenting both mental retardation and a dwarfed stature.

24 *Seneb and family: the dwarfed arms and legs of the head of the household can be clearly seen. Seneb's children and wife are of normal stature. Sixth Dynasty.*

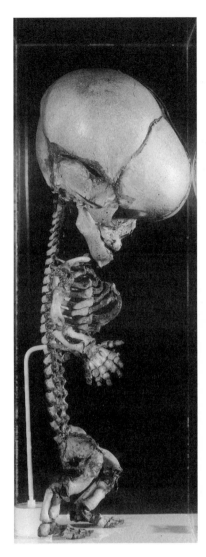 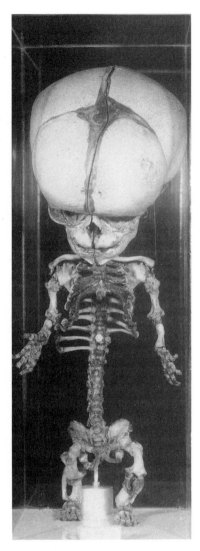

25, 26 *Side and front views of an infant achondroplastic skeleton (non-Egyptian) showing the full extent of the disorder.*

Egypt is a major source of skeletal evidence for achondroplasia in the ancient world. A complete skeleton from predynastic Badari and a single humerus from the tomb of King Djer (early First Dynasty) are both considered to be examples of the condition. There are also two early dynastic skeletons from the tomb of King Semerkhet attributed to achondroplasia: one consists of short squat bones only, whilst the other also includes a skull with a depressed nasal area, a short skull base and a broad face. Recent research in Egypt suggests that there was a burial area near the Giza pyramids for high-ranking Old Kingdom dwarfs. Near Seneb's tomb at Giza archaeologists have found the tomb and skeleton of Perenankh, a statue of whom

27 *This depiction of a female dwarf from the tomb of Tutankhamun (Eighteenth Dynasty) reminds us that both women and men could be affected by achondroplasia.*

was discussed in Chapter 2. Perenankh was a court official during the Fifth or Sixth Dynasty and his skeleton has revealed that he was about 40 years old when he died. Unfortunately the facial part of his skull is missing but the rest of his skeleton shows the unmistakeable traits of achondroplasia: squat, robust upper and lower limbs. An interesting skull found at the temple of Tuthmosis IV at Thebes is now thought to be that of an achondroplastic female in her early twenties, though Seligmann originally considered it to belong to a cretin. The skeleton of another female achondroplastic dwarf reveals poignantly her cause of death. Modern medical treatment recommends Caesarean section for the safe delivery of a child of an achondroplastic female. Unfortunately such help was not available for this woman,

28 *Amuletic figures showing features of achondroplasia.*

29 *Below right: an Egyptian achondroplastic right femur (a cast) of Old Kingdom date. Left: a normally-sized Nubian left femur for comparison.*

a member of the workmen's community near Giza, and she died before her child was delivered. The child's remains were in situ when the body was discovered.

Artistic evidence for dwarfism is well established from ancient Egypt. In addition to the Seneb family already mentioned there is a Fifth Dynasty limestone statue of Khnumhotep which shows not only the shortened limbs and disproportionate nature of the condition but also the skull shape associated with achondroplasia. Other examples include a Late Dynastic depiction of the dwarf Djedher on his sarcophagus lid from Saqqara, now in the Cairo Museum, the lower half of a particularly well-sculpted statue in the museum at Memphis and the statue of the nobleman Perenankh from Giza. The skull and facial features of Perenankh's statue are normal but his arms and legs are typically foreshortened and, as mentioned previously, their measurements seem to concur with those of the skeleton.

There are a variety of other depictions of achondroplastic dwarfs in Egyptian art. One of the earliest drawings, known as the dwarf of Djer, is on a bowl of metamorphic rock from Abydos. Dwarfs are illustrated in Late Period funerary papyrus vignettes (Chapter 164) and on tomb walls. From these tomb decorations we see the types of activities dwarfs engaged in. They often tended animals, especially the pets of their wealthy masters. On the west wall of the tomb of Serfka (father of Werireni) at Sheikh Said, a dwarf servant stands beside his master's chair holding a pet ape by a leash. In another scene in the same tomb a dwarf is leading a greyhound. In the Eleventh Dynasty tomb of Khety (tomb no. 17) at Beni Hasan, two dwarfs named Seneb and Nemu stand beside the tomb owner and, on an outer door lintel in the tomb of Panehesy, dwarfs are seen in attendance on the Amarna royal family as they worship the sun. In a

fishing scene in the tomb of Inti at Deshasha men are busy dragging nets whilst on the prow of the boat a dwarf stands, his right arm uplifted, brandishing a sling. No doubt because of their great strength dwarfs are often seen carrying objects. In a drawing from Athribis a dwarf (probably female) carries a large object on her head, her short squat figure contrasting greatly with the slim female walking in front of her. Another dwarf, this one male, carries a large rectangular object on his head in a scene from Deshasha. This figure also holds a necklace in his right hand for it was at jewellery making that dwarfs were mainly employed. In the same scene (Tomb of Inti, Deshasha) another dwarf is occupied assembling jewellery at the work table. In the Tomb of Nefer (mid-Fifth Dynasty) at Saqqara a scene shows some dwarfs making necklaces. One holds the necklace

30 *A small figurine of Khnumhotep, an achondroplastic dwarf who achieved courtly status during the Old Kingdom.*

31 *The lid from the sarcophagus of Djedher depicts the owner (probably at near-life size) as a dwarf.*

32 *Dwarfs were often depicted tending pets such as dogs or apes as shown here, from the tomb of Serfka at Sheikh Said.*

whilst his companion threads on more beads.

The evidence offered by Egyptian art seems to point to a prominence of achondroplastic dwarfs in ancient Egypt, and has led one researcher to suggest that there was a high mutation rate amongst the populace. In fact modern incidence of this condition is in the order of one per ten thousand live births and was likely to have been so in antiquity. Throughout history many royal families in many countries have taken dwarfs into their households and this seems to have been the case in ancient Egypt. It was sometimes the case that the achondroplastic dwarf's unusual physique caught the attention of a

33 *Fishing scene from the tomb of Inti. The dwarfed figure on the extreme left of the boat seems to be in charge of the work.*

royal patron so he or she was raised to some prominence in the household. Such dwarves were therefore often depicted in tomb scenes of daily life, so their numbers might appear to have been abundant. As the condition is not associated with mental retardation there is every expectation that such individuals contributed usefully to society. Indeed, some dwarfs achieved high status: Khnumhotep, according to Maspero, was 'Chief of the Perfumes' and 'Head of the Wardrobe', and this latter title was also accorded to Seneb who was mentioned at the beginning of this chapter. Perenankh was 'Administrator of the Treasury'. The costly tombs of Seneb, Khnumhotep and Perenankh and the granite sarcophagus (with its inscription) of Djedher also point to their exalted position in Egyptian society.

When reviewing the evidence for dwarfism in ancient Egypt we cannot overlook the appearance of two gods. One of the roles of Ptah was as the patron god of craftsmen. This was no doubt derived from the belief that the deity created artisan skills. Usually this anthropomorphic god is dressed in a tight garment (like a mummy) which emphasises his streamlined figure but, according to Herodotus, his physique could also echo that of the excellent dwarfish craftsmen with characteristic bowed legs and short stature. In fact, such images (now called *pataikoi*) are more closely connected with the protective figure of Horus-the-child triumphing over noxious creatures found on magical plaques known as *cippi*.

Brandishing his knife, the short stocky figure of Bes, a dwarf helper at childbirth, is a familiar one. He is usually depicted mustachioed with a lion's mane emphasising his ferocious attitude. Abnormally short lower and upper limbs with broad 'squared-off' extremities,

34 *Dwarfs were often depicted making jewellery as in this scene, from the mastaba of Mereruka (Sixth Dynasty, Saqqara).*

35 *Chair or bed strut depicting the god Bes. The figure of this benign god was often incorporated into furniture as it was believed by the Egyptians that he brought good luck to the home. Bes had the stature of a dwarf.*

infantile genitalia and a robust stature are the usual features of Bes and clearly declare him to be an achondroplastic dwarf. His tongue protruding in a roguish manner, he is depicted as lively and intelligent. This lively nature is also seen in images of Bes making noise. Whilst the usual skull features of dwarfism are not depicted in figures of Bes, quite often a depressed nasal bridge is apparent. Despite his grotesque appearance Bes was benign in character and his main role was as a protector at childbirth, chasing away evil with his knife. Here the making of noise is an important factor in driving off less well-intentioned demons. His figure, often incorporated into household items such as beds and chairs, brought prosperity and protection to the home.

There are representations of Bes in various media, many of which had amuletic connotations. One fine representation is a wooden figure in the British Museum. The figure is 27 cm in height and is exceptionally well carved. On the grounds of style and workmanship the figure is probably from the Eighteenth Dynasty. Made from tamarisk wood, the item was originally a decorative strut from a chair or a bed. In addition to the expected features of achondroplasia, there has been a realistic attempt to model details. Thus, leg and arm muscles are well-defined, the breasts are slightly pronounced and the nasal area is carved to produce a depressed bridge.

OTHER CONGENITAL DISORDERS

Tutankhamun's tomb contained two foetuses embalmed and enclosed in miniature anthropoid coffins, found when the so-called Treasury was cleared in 1926. It is likely that these were Tutankhamun's own children by his wife Ankhesenamun. The first foetus, probably a female, was of no more than five months' gestation, the second, a female, was of about eight or nine months' gestation. When this second body was X-rayed it was found that the baby had suffered from scoliosis (curvature of the spine), spina bifida and Sprengel's deformity (which had affected the baby's left shoulder blade congenitally). In a Sprengel deformity the shoulder blade is pushed up or elevated and it may affect one or both shoulder blades. The condition can recur in several generations of a family but most cases occur sporadically.

Osteogenesis imperfecta, another congenital disorder, is a condition arising from an inadequate formation of bone tissue. This results in brittle and delicate bones and is often referred to in modern times as 'brittle bone' disease. In one of its forms, osteogenesis imperfecta fetalis, the condition develops within the womb and before a foetus is born it may already have fractured many or all the bones in its body (plate VI). In modern times such infants are delivered by Caesarean

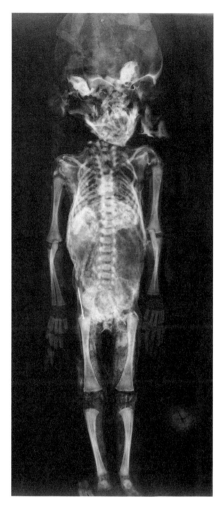

36 *A foetus, possibly a daughter of Tutankhamun (Eighteenth Dynasty).*

37 *X-ray of the foetus showing the elevated left scapula (a Sprengel's deformity) and scoliosis (curvature) of the spine.*

section as the very act of birth could fracture all the bones in the body, but in ancient times it is unlikely that many survived the trauma of birth. The second form of the disorder, osteogenesis imperfecta tarda, appears during childhood or adolescence and leads to many fractures. Those who may have survived into adulthood would have endured life as an invalid and all but the most sedentary of occupations would have been denied them for fear of casual knocks or blows resulting in fractures.

Extant examples of skeletons from antiquity showing this condition are rare. Children's skeletons do not survive well and the very fragile nature of bones with osteogenesis imperfecta makes their survival even more unlikely. To date, there are only three archaeological examples of the disease in the world. One of these, an Anglo-Saxon, is uncertain, the evidence resting on only a single deformed left femur. The second example is part of the skeleton of a Nubian child in the pathology collection at the Natural History Museum, London, and the third, from ancient Egypt, is part of the Egyptian collection at the British Museum. This infant and its coffin were found at Speos Artimedos and on the evidence of decoration and workmanship Dr J. H. Taylor in the Department of Egyptian Antiquities has dated it to the Twenty-second Dynasty. Naturally the coffin played an important part in protecting the bones of this very fragile individual, and the skull and nearly complete post-cranial remains show unequivocal evidence of the disease. The skull, on display at the British Museum, shows what is sometimes referred to as the 'Tam O'Shanter' effect associated with this disease: the weight of the vault cannot be supported so it settles into a beret-like shape. The post-cranial remains of this infant are light and friable, the bones having a 'biscuit-like' texture, and many of them, especially in the upper and lower limbs, are distorted due to massive fracturing. The teeth, which show particular symptoms related to the disease, are discussed in the chapter on dental health.

One of the most severe and distressing congenital abnormalities is anencephaly, a fatal malformation of the skull. In this condition the skull does not develop during foetal growth, and the neural canal may not close so any rudimentary brain is exposed and life after birth is not possible. The cause of the condition is likely to be genetic but other factors cannot be ruled out. It is possible that the disorder was equally as common in antiquity as in modern times – an incidence of around one per thousand – but the rarity of evidence makes this purely a tentative suggestion. Perhaps the best known example of anencephaly comes from the Catacombs of Hermopolis in Egypt. Originally thought to be the mummy of an ape, as these catacombs were indeed the burial place for such animals, it is now known to be an anencephalic infant.

The deformity of the left foot of the Pharaoh Siptah (Nineteenth Dynasty) is thought to be due to poliomyelitis, but clubfoot is a possible alternative. Clubfoot (talipes equinovarus) is a condition where one or both feet are congenitally formed into an inverted position causing difficulty in walking. Experts differ in opinion as to the frequency of clubfoot in antiquity as the defect is difficult to identify. It is often confused with post-paralytic deformities such as those associated with poliomyelitis. In 1910 the mummy of the Twelfth Dynasty priest Khnumnakht was unwrapped by Margaret Murray (see Chapter 3). Khnumnakht was diagnosed as having a marked degree of talipes equinovarus in the left foot, but a recent re-examination of his foot now suggests that the bandages (tightly wrapped during mummification) produced features similar to club-

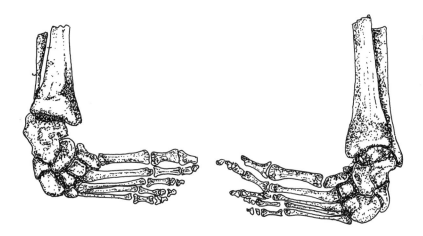

38 *Inverted bones of the feet, a feature of talipes equinovarus (clubfoot).*

foot, and the original diagnosis of clubfoot now seems unlikely.

Representational art from ancient Egypt also seems to give fairly clear evidence for talipes equinovarus. Tomb paintings at Beni Hasan from the Eleventh and Twelfth Dynasties depict two people with clubfeet. That both of these individuals are young emphasises the fact that the condition develops early in life. Two female figures from Amarna have clubfeet and it seems likely that they were also dwarfs. Drawings from tombs at Deshasha also show figures with inverted feet, the classic feature of the condition.

Two abnormalities which affect parts of the skull are cleft palate and hydrocephalus. A cleft palate develops in the womb when the two halves of the palate fail to unite, leaving an opening (which may occur unilaterally or bilaterally) connecting the oral and nasal cavities. In modern times the incidence of cleft palate is one per thousand live births and this may have been true for ancient societies. The condition is not genetic in origin and there are a variety of environmental factors which may lead to its occurrence. Today, the condition may be corrected surgically but in ancient times the severely afflicted, unable to be nursed or fed, would often die. That some individuals with cleft palate survived into adulthood is an indication of the extreme care their parents must have taken. Some ancient societies in South America revered individuals with cleft palate and depicted them on pots. In many societies, however, the deformed child was allowed to die either because of superstitious beliefs that an 'evil eye' had been cast on the child, or because of the serious practical difficulties in feeding.

Unlike a cleft palate, the combined occurrence of cleft palate with a cleft (or hare) lip is genetic in origin in seventy-five per cent of cases. The cleft lip defect occurs between the lateral incisor and the canine

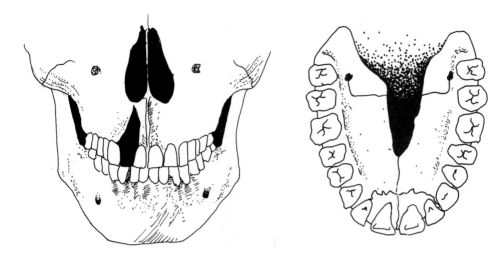

39 *A cleft (hare) lip.*

40 *Cleft palate. The bones of the palate have failed to unite.*

tooth and has an incidence of one in six hundred live births.

Individuals with cleft palates surviving into adulthood would have suffered a marked degree of facial disfigurement and would have had difficulty in producing intelligible speech. Without a palate the tongue is unable to articulate correctly and the oral cavity cannot act as a resonator in speech production. Thus, in antiquity, the cleft palate sufferer had to contend with both facial disfigurement and difficulty in communicating with friends and family.

Archaeological examples of cleft palate and/or cleft lip are not common as the mortality rate for such infants would have been high. One complete skull of an adult woman from the Nubian pathology collection at the Natural History Museum, London, shows how the bilateral condition has affected the central and posterior parts of the palate, leaving it open to the nasal cavity. Another skull exhibiting a deformed palate was excavated by Brunton in a cemetery on the east bank of the Nile, some thirty miles south of Asyut. The skull, from a Twenty-fifth Dynasty grave, belongs to a woman beyond middle age at death. The lower jaw projects beyond the maxilla (upper jaw) and the pre-maxillary portion of the maxilla is absent, as are the incisor teeth. These examples together with another female with cleft palate of Roman date indicate the caring attitude of friends and family.

Hydrocephalus occurs when the fluid-containing spaces within the brain expand, resulting in an abnormally large head. The condition is commonly known as 'water on the brain'. The vault increases in all directions and takes on a globular shape. In antiquity the enlarged head of an afflicted infant would have obstructed labour and both mother and child were likely to die in childbirth. Any extant archaeological examples of people with hydrocephalus were likely therefore to have developed the condition shortly after being born. The term hydrocephalus describes only the abnormality not the cause. There are a variety of possible causes for the disease: a tumour within the skull, a viral infection of the brain substance, parasitic infection or perinatal trauma.

A child's skull exhibiting hydrocephalic changes was found during the excavation of a Nubian cemetery dating from between AD 300 and 500. Possibly one of the better-known archaeological examples of the condition is of Roman date and was found by Engelbach in a cemetery at Shurafa near Helwan. The hydrocephalic skull and the extant post-cranial remains belong to a man of at least 30 years of age and the skull's cranial capacity of 2901.4 cubic centimetres exceeds the normal capacity by several hundred cubic centimetres. As the occipital (or posterior) area of his skull does not have any Wormian (or extra) bones along the suture lines it is likely that the skull was fully developed before the onset of the hydrocephaly; although he could have been exposed to its causes early in life. It has been argued that he suffered from a partial left hemiplegia (a paralysis or stroke). Upon examination the left upper and lower limb bones were seen to be far less developed than the right. It would seem that the paralysis was brought about by excessive pressure on the motor-function areas of the right brain hemisphere. This Egyptian of the Roman period would have walked only with the aid of a staff and his occupation and lifestyle would have been severely restricted.

CHAPTER FIVE

Acquired Disorders

Human disease is a reaction by the individual to his or her environment and in Chapter 1 some of the factors which promoted disease in ancient Egypt were outlined. Whilst some of the diseases in ancient Egypt were undeniably serious and severely affected the sufferer, others were an accepted part of every-day life.

Not all diseases leave evidence of their existence on human remains. Certain types of illnesses, such as fevers, resolve themselves quickly, by subsiding or by killing the patient, and leave no identifiable traces on the body. Chest infections, boils and many serious skin problems which affect the soft tissues of the body remain unrecorded, as do the more dangerous complaints such as meningitis which resolve themselves too quickly (by recovery or death) to leave any tell-tale signs behind. It is important not to underestimate the occurrence of such conditions in ancient times.

TUBERCULOSIS

Ancient Egypt gives us some of the earliest evidence for tuberculosis from the ancient world. There are several related types of the tubercle bacillus, including those which affected cold-blooded animals and birds, but it was the bovine and human strain which threatened the health of the ancient Egyptian. As already discussed, people were vulnerable to disease caught from domesticated animals, and as the peoples of the Near East were the first to bring animals into domestic life, it is here that we would expect to find the earliest evidence of such diseases. One of the earliest examples of spinal tuberculosis has been found at excavations at the predynastic site of Adaima, 8 km south of Esna. The skeleton, that of a female, has a well-defined kyphosis

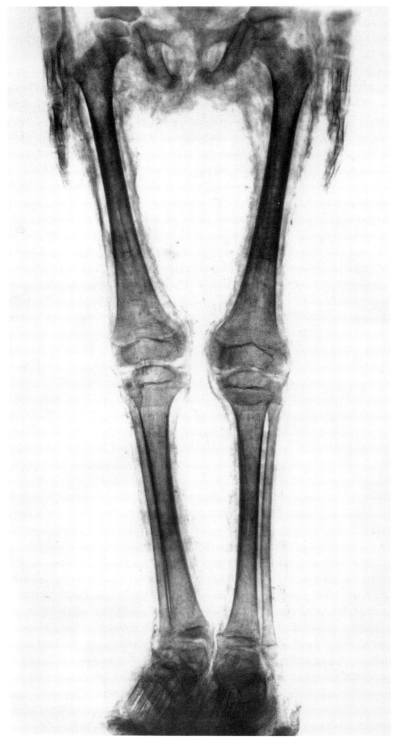

41 *X-ray of mummy in fig. 42. Lines of arrested growth (Harris lines) at the ends of the leg bones suggest the child had undergone periods of stress. A further examination of the body revealed she had suffered from tuberculosis.*

42 *Mummy of a Ptolemaic child, now in Bolton Museum. An X-ray can be seen in fig. 41.*

of the spine which may well be attributable to tuberculosis.

Many Egyptian paintings testify to the growing relationship between man and his animals, both as breeding stock and as pets. The breeding of cattle is well attested from both paintings and tomb models and bovine tuberculosis spreads secondarily to humans through infected milk or meat. The human strain of tuberculosis is extremely contagious. The infected person coughs and spreads bacilli from an active area of infection, which is often the lungs. In the body the bacilli can travel to other parts of the system causing tuberculosis of the lymph nodes, kidneys, intestines and other organs, but evidence of diseased soft tissue from the past is rare. In some cases the bacilli enter the growth centres of the bone, affecting its development, and many archaeological examples of this type of tuberculosis may be found.

Spinal tuberculosis, or Pott's disease, is a common and characteristic form of the disease and is the one more likely to be found in archaeological contexts. The infection causes an inflammatory reaction, bone is destroyed, and between two and four vertebrae in the lower thoracic area can collapse producing an angular kyphosis or hump. Pott's disease is well attested, in both Egyptian art and in human remains. Several clay statuettes, thought to be predynastic in date, perhaps depict spinal tuberculosis. The figures, some of which are in clay bowls, show an emaciated body, a drawn face and a humped back, and were discussed more fully in Chapter 2 (fig. 11).

A wooden figurine in Brussels Museum, again thought to be of predynastic date, shows both an angular kyphosis of the spine and an angular projection of the chest, which is another feature associated with Pott's disease. A Nineteenth Dynasty depiction of a gardener raising water with a *shaduf* is also considered to be a case of spinal tuberculosis and has been discussed in Chapter 2 (fig. 12).

Human remains provide evidence of tuberculosis from many periods of ancient Egypt. A 4–6 year old girl, whose mummy is in Bolton Museum, appears to have had spinal tuberculosis (see fig. 41). Probably the most famous case from Egypt is that of

 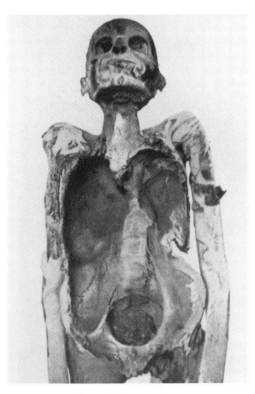

44 *Nespaheran, a priest of Amun from the Twenty-First Dynasty. Left: side view showing a marked kyphotic (humped) spine. Right: the front wall of the mummy removed to show an abscess in the right psoas muscle.*

Nespaheran, an adult male discovered by Grébaut amongst a group of mummies found at Thebes in 1891. They were the well-preserved bodies of priests and priestesses of Amun from the Twenty-first Dynasty. The mummy of Nespaheran shows the characteristic angular deformity which results when the lower thoracic and upper lumbar vertebrae have been partially destroyed. During an examination, the front body wall was removed and an abscess in the right psoas muscle was detected. Such abscesses are often a later symptom of spinal tuberculosis.

In 1991 the tomb of Iurudef at Saqqara was excavated by the joint mission of the Egypt Exploration Society and the Leiden Museum of Antiquities. Iurudef was an important official in the household of Princess Tia, sister of Pharaoh Ramesses II of the Nineteenth Dynasty. In the excavation report R. Walker describes an intrusive burial of a non-royal female in Iurudef's tomb. The woman, who had died aged about twenty, had extensive spinal degeneration resulting in a marked kyphosis, with a possible paravertebral abscess. There is reason to believe that the woman had lived her life as an invalid and only survived through family care.

Tuberculosis thrives in dense urban living conditions, where it is transmitted easily from person to person. As we saw in the chapter on the environment some households in ancient Egypt may have been overcrowded providing the ideal conditions for the spread of disease.

LEPROSY

It was not until 1882 that Robert Koch discovered the tuberculosis bacillus, and it was even later before it was realised that there are several strains. The bacillus which causes leprosy belongs to the same group and there is an identifiable historical relationship between the two diseases.

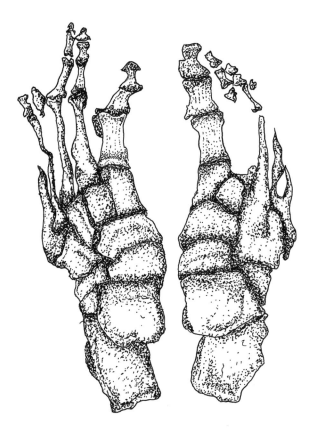

45 *Bones of the feet, showing typical changes to the toes caused by leprosy.*

Throughout history few diseases have provoked such stigma and cruelty as leprosy, and it has been described as unique in its ability to generate fear. Leprosy is a chronic infectious disease caused by the spread of *Mycobacterium leprae*, the leprosy bacillus. Because leprosy and tuberculosis are of the same genus there is some cross-immunity and a decrease in the incidence of leprosy in an increasingly urbanised population may be accompanied by a growing number of cases of tuberculosis.

Unlike tuberculosis, leprosy attacks the body in specific areas.

I *The naturally dessicated body of an adolescent (c.3200 BC). Tests on samples of skin have revealed early evidence of schistosomiasis.*

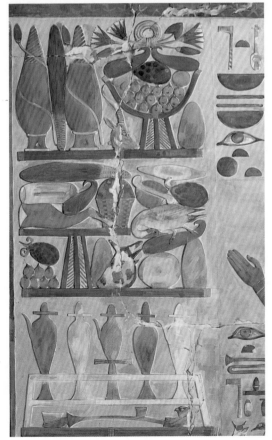

II *A detail from Howard Carter's water-colour copy of Egyptian food depicted on a wall painting from Eighteenth-Dynasty Thebes, c.1450 BC.*

III *The hair and skin from many Egyptian and Nubian bodies survives and can be tested for information about diet and disease. This is an adult female found at Gabati, Sudan. Post-Meroitic period (c.400–500 AD).*

IV *A nineteenth-century painting by Phillipoteaux showing an autopsy of an Egyptian mummy in progress. In the course of the work the mummy was destroyed.*

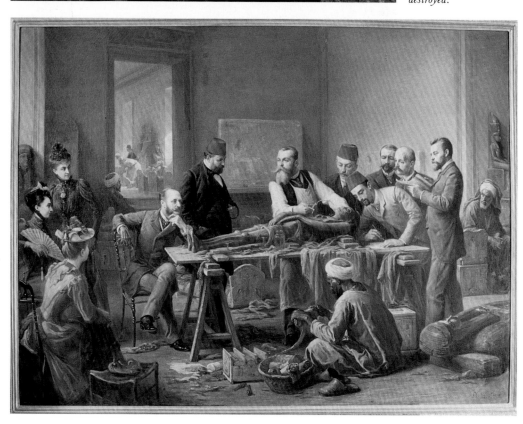

V *Xero-radiograph showing the animal bone and seeds used to pack the nose of Ramesses II (Nineteenth Dynasty) during mummification. These prevented the nose being flattened by the linen bandages.*

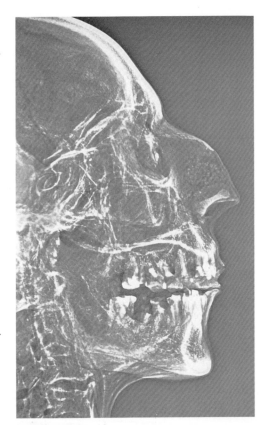

VI *Two infant leg bones. The distortion due to fracturing shows that the child suffered from osteogenesis imperfecta or brittle bone disease.*

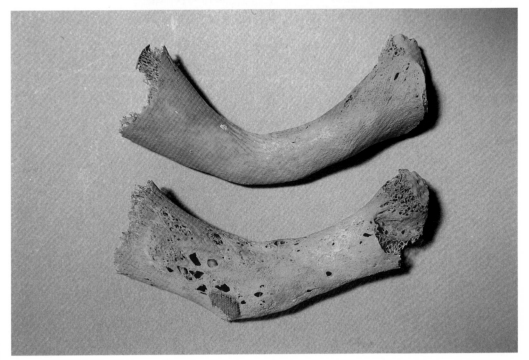

VII *A group of Sudanese children. One boy has a withered leg and can walk only by clutching his knee. The deformity is probably due to poliomyelitis.*

VIII *Two arm bones, the right one broken midshaft. The injury has healed leaving it slightly shorter than the left. Gabati, Sudan (*c.*300 BC–400 AD).*

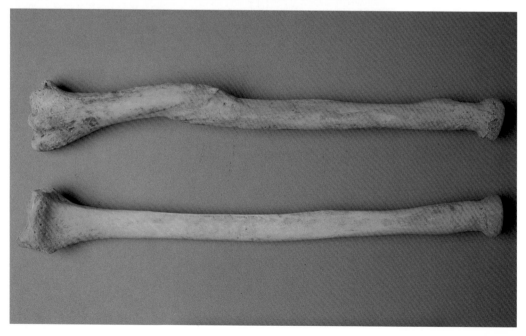

Characteristic symptoms are mutilated hands and feet with the fingers and toes reduced to stumps, collapse of the nasal bridge, missing upper central incisors and ulcerated eyes which will eventually go blind. In antiquity the leprous person was a sorry sight indeed with a persistant nasal discharge from the destroyed nasal area and a hoarse, rasping voice as the throat and larynx were invaded by bacteria. It is easy to understand why people fled from the leper for fear of catching the disease.

Leprosy is known to be infectious, yet some researchers now suggest that it is relatively difficult to transmit the disease and prolonged exposure is needed in order to catch it. Thus leprosy was commonly a family disease and incidences of whole families being affected are reported in the Bible. The disease can be contracted by inhaling droplets which the sick person has sneezed out of his nose. Once contracted, the bacilli travel along the nervous system causing areas of anaesthesia. They then invade the skin, nodules form and as they invade the bloodstream the circulation is inhibited.

There has been much speculation about the early history of leprosy. Whilst one of the earliest written records giving an accurate description of the disease is from India, dating from about 600 BC, the earliest skeletal evidence comes from Egypt. In 1980 a Ptolemaic cemetery at Balat in the Dakhleh oasis revealed four adult male skeletons, and T. Dzierzykray-Rogalski argued that they showed changes typical of leprosy: atrophy of the nasal spine resulting in the collapse of the nose, perforation of the palate and the loss of the upper incisor teeth. Importantly, according to Dzierzykray-Rogalski, these four men were of European type, buried in a cemetery whose skeletons had predominantly 'negroid' features leading researchers to suggest that they had been banished there from Alexandria

46 *Hands (left) and feet (right) of a Coptic mummy (Nubia, Sixth century AD). The fingers and toes have been reduced to stumps by leprosy.*

because they were lepers. If this was so then it suggests that the ancient Egyptians had had previous experience of the disease and knew that its contagious nature could only be controlled through isolation. As the disease takes from two to eight years to incubate, the Egyptians must have had sufficient experience of it in order to become acquainted with its infectious nature. Consequently, it is likely that more examples of the disease will come to light.

Much later evidence of the disease has been found in the Coptic cemetery on the island of Biga, near Philae. Dating to the fourth century AD two bodies, one male and one female, exhibit the mutilated hands and feet and destruction of the facial area typical of leprosy. Another possible case has been identified in a collection of Egyptian remains now in Cambridge.

Despite the horrific nature of leprosy it was rarely the cause of death in itself. The loss of sensation in the digits meant they were in danger of being burnt, allowing an often fatal infection to set in. Life for a leprous ancient Egyptian would have been one of hideous deformity and isolation from home, family and friends.

POLIOMYELITIS

Another infectious disease, the early evidence for which comes from Egypt, is poliomyelitis (plate VII). A limestone funerary stele

47 *A New Kingdom stele showing the doorkeeper Roma with an atrophied leg due to poliomyelitis.*

48 *A Twelfth Dynasty stele in the British Museum. Again, like Roma (fig. 47) the tomb owner leans on a staff, and his left leg appears thinner than the right.*

from the Eighteenth Dynasty in Copenhagen shows that the right leg of Roma, doorkeeper for the Lady Yamia, was atrophied after paralytic poliomyelitis. Polio is a viral infection of the central nervous system which manifests itself in the paralysis of one or more muscle groups. Polio occurs more frequently during early life and so is often known as infantile paralysis. The paralysis of an upper or lower limb results in muscle wasting and impaired growth. Roma is portrayed with lower limbs of unequal length and he walks aided by a staff. Despite his infirmity he attained a responsible position in life and on his stele he is accompanied by his wife and child. Another stele in the British Museum may also be an attempt to depict an atrophied leg.

TUMOURS

Modern opinion might suggest that tumours are a disease of advanced industrial societies only. Tumours or neoplastic growths are uncontrolled expansions of tissue cells within the body. Usually these growths are not restricted to any particular age, sex, or ethnic or socio-economic group. Whilst there is not a huge amount of ancient Egyptian evidence for such bone changes, there is enough to suggest that tumours did occur in antiquity and are not exclusively a problem of modern life.

Neoplastic growths can occur in the soft tissues of the body but archaeological evidence for these is rare. Sandison described a squamous papilloma on the hand of a Late Dynastic mummy. Elliot Smith and Wood Jones recorded a Byzantine Nubian mummy with a vaginal cyst. As mentioned in Chapter 2 Granville originally diagnosed a case of ovarian dropsy (cancer) in the mummy of an elderly woman, but uterine samples examined by Dr E. Tapp indicate a benign cyst – not as dangerous or life threatening, but certainly the oldest known example. Sometimes a tumour of the soft tissue may produce a reaction in the bone which resembles a neoplasm. A meningioma, which is a growth of the membranes covering the brain, can grow to startling dimensions, as was seen in a skull from Meydum dating from the Twentieth Dynasty which has a honeycomb-like mass on the top.

There is slightly more evidence for tumours of the bony skeleton. Bone tumour types are either benign or malignant. Benign tumours (such as osteomas, osteochondromas) remain at the site of origin and spread only locally, but can sometimes look quite formidable as in a famous Fifth Dynasty femur with osteochondroma, where the cartilage has developed in the growing period of the skeleton into an irregular bony mass with a dry-bone appearance. Despite its appearance this tumour was harmless. A large chondroblastic tumour occurs at the head end of a Nubian humerus, now in the

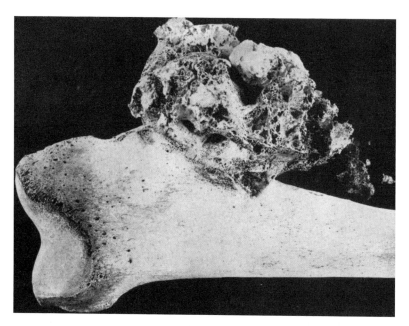

49 *A Fifth Dynasty femur showing an enormous outgrowth of bone typical of osteochondroma.*

Natural History Museum, London. Osteomas are also commonly seen in the archaeological record. They are mounds of compact bone which usually occur on the frontal or parietal area of the skull. A particularly large osteoma occurs on the right side of an Egyptian skull of Roman date. More recently one was found on a skull of medieval date from Soba in Sudan.

Malignant bone tumours are usually fatal and are characterised by an uncontrolled spread of a primary lesion via the bloodstream into other areas (or organs) of the body. P. Podzorski mentions a possible case of a malignant tumour where destruction was seen on the left side of skull of a woman from predynastic Naga-ed-Der. She may have been blind in her left eye as a result of this lesion. Dr E. Strouhal has reported an Old Kingdom case of naso-pharyngeal cancer in a middle-aged man found in the same cemetery. He also describes malignant lesions in the skull of a woman from the sixth- to eleventh-century AD cemetery at Sayala in Egyptian Nubia. As tumours are often a feature of the elderly and as ancient Egyptian life expectancy was short, we may not expect to see many cases of such tumours.

Textual evidence for tumours may be found in the Ebers Papyrus, which includes a reference to such symptoms as 'an eating lesion' and 'a glandular swelling'. The Hearst Papyrus contains similar references. Turning to artistic evidence several reliefs in Old Kingdom mastaba tombs at Saqqara show various types of 'swellings'. The tomb of the vizier Mehu has depictions of scrotal hernias, umbilical hernias and gynaecomastia (swellings of the breast area). Ptah-

50 *An Old Kingdom statue, in Cairo Museum, suggesting the protruding eyes and thickened neck associated with Graves' disease.*

Hetep's tomb chapel shows a similar range of umbilical and genital hernias. Dr P. Ghalioungui has suggested that the hernias and gynaecomastia may in fact be tumours. However, such symptoms might also indicate infestation by parasites such as the schistosome which can also result in swellings.

ENDOCRINE AND METABOLIC DISORDERS

A variety of diseases can be acquired when endocrine or metabolic disorders arise. Endocrine diseases result from abnormal activity of the ductless glands. There is a chemical change in the hormones they secrete, which affects how the body's metabolism behaves. An iodine deficiency produces under-activity in the thyroid gland resulting in cretinism and dwarfism in children. Over-activity of the thyroid ductless glands, however, leads to Graves' disease, also known as exophthalmia. The face of a statue from the Old Kingdom, now in the Cairo Museum, seems to show the features of the disease: a full, thick neck, protruding eyes and a strained expression. A dysfunction of the pituitary gland also produces disorders, some of which can damage the skeleton. The most famous and most controversial example of a possible pituitary disorder is that of Pharaoh Akhenaten. Certain statues of the king showing an excessively jutting lower jaw and thickened brow ridges have led to the suggestion that he suffered from acromegaly (an overgrowth of the hands, feet and face), resulting from a pituitary problem but, as we saw in the section on artistic sources, without the king's body we can only speculate.

Metabolic disorders can arise from chemical changes other than those in the ductless glands. Gout, a metabolic disease well known in eighteenth-century England, has also been found in an Egyptian context. Gout is caused by an excess of uric acid in the blood which is deposited in the joint tissues as crystals with damaging results. Archaeological evidence of gout is rare, but the most famous example is that of a mummy of the Coptic period from the island of Philae. The mummy is that of an old man with long white hair and beard, whose joints showed concentrations of the urate salts typical of gout. Writings from eighteenth-century England describe the gout sufferer as irritable and bad-tempered due to the severe pain of the condition. The destructive nature of gout eventually leads to arthritis, one of the most commonly occurring conditions in ancient times.

Joint Diseases

Joint diseases are a group of abnormalities which are related but have different causes, some of which are unknown. As shown above, a metabolically related form of arthritis can occur as a consequence of gout. Septic arthritis is caused by blood-borne bacteria entering the joint cavities (usually the hip or knee joints) or through a wound. Infection sets in, and cartilage is destroyed and the bone becomes damaged. The causes of rheumatoid arthritis are still not fully understood. This disease is known to inflame and disfigure joints and tends to occur in the fourth and fifth decades of life. As other organs of the body are affected it may not be correct to term it solely a joint disease. Evidence for rheumatoid arthritis in antiquity is in short supply but a Fifth Dynasty skeleton of a middle-aged man excavated by Petrie at Deshasha shows some arthritic changes to the spine. As with tumours, rheumatoid arthritis is a feature of the later years of life and the short life expectancy of most ancient Egyptians has meant that it is not well represented in the archaeological record.

Ankylosing spondylitis, sometimes known as 'bamboo spine', is a

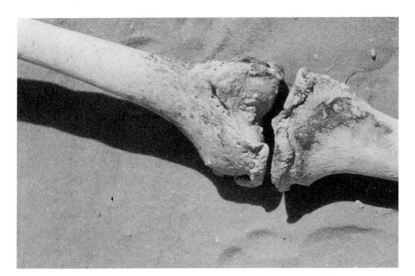

51 *A knee joint showing arthritic changes, possibly with some septic complications. Gabati, Sudan. (Meroitic period).*

severely crippling degenerative disease whose cause is unknown. In contrast to rheumatoid arthritis, it more commonly affects men than women. Onset of the disease is usually during the second or third decade of life, and after the joints have become inflamed the spine becomes progressively fixed until the whole vertebral column becomes immobile. Sometimes even the joints of the pelvis and ribs are affected, resulting in severe disability, ever increasing back pain and stiffness. Eventually, total immobilisation leaves the sufferer unable to work and dependent on their community or family for support. Several cases of ankylosing spondylitis have been described from both Egypt and Nubia. An adult man from Third Dynasty Egypt had his whole spine fused, as did an adult Nubian man. Partial fixing of the spine has been found in the bodies of several ancient Nubians and in a predynastic body from Hierakonpolis.

As people age so their bodies deteriorate and eventually the bodily systems break down. Osteoarthritis affects the synovial joints such as the knee and is acquired through advancing age or stress. As the joint is continually used, the cartilage wears away leaving bones rubbing together without any cushioning between them. Under this stress the bone ends develop lipping at the edges. Osteoarthritis is mainly associated with ageing, but the study of joints commonly affected in ancient times may provide insights into the occupations of the sufferers. The agricultural worker, for example, who was continually bending and lifting, would be far more likely to develop traumatic osteoarthritis than those with sedentary occupations, but it should be stressed that an association between osteoarthritis and types of work is difficult to prove.

Another condition which affects the spine is osteophytosis. Man is

52 *Part of a spine with osteophytic growths, Gabati, Sudan.*

subject to developing osteophytes (bony outgrowths on the spinal bodies) because he is an upright bipedal creature. Stress (and wear and tear through ageing) on the vertebral bodies causes the discs between them to rupture, stimulating the growth of bone from the edges of the vertebral body, allowing the load to be redistributed over a wider area, rather like shock absorbers. As the amount of stress increases so the osteophytes grow in size. Research on modern people has shown that by the fifth decade of life some degree of osteophytosis is present in over sixty per cent of the spines studied. By the ninth decade almost everybody has developed osteophytosis. As with osteoarthritis, the distribution and severity of the disorder may tentatively indicate the roles (or occupations) of individuals within a society. Heavy manual labour involving bending and lifting puts strain on the back. Scenes of Egyptian farmers tending their fields and workers lifting heavy objects illustrate how the spine was subjected to stress.

MALARIA

As we saw in the discussion of the environment, a variety of parasites can attack the human body. Internal parasites such as the schistosome (and the hookworm) cause internal damage and a massive loss of blood, resulting in debilitating anaemia. One of the world's oldest external human parasites is the mosquito, which infects man with malaria when feeding on his blood. Malarial infection is caused by the female Anopheles mosquito transmitting the plasmodium parasite when withdrawing human blood. The usual pattern of the disease involves the periodic destruction of thousands of red blood cells which results in intermittent fevers in the human host as a response to the plasmodia moving through the bloodstream. Herodotus' comments on the annoyance caused by gnats in Upper and Lower Egypt were outlined earlier. If these gnats are identified as mosquitoes then we have a case for the probable existence of malaria in ancient Egypt. Until recently there was little biological evidence to support this, but new research by R. Miller and colleagues on the Granville mummy at the British Museum has revealed that the lady, in addition to having pneumonia and an ovarian cyst, may have also suffered from malaria.

CHAPTER SIX

Trauma

Trauma can include a variety of conditions which provide a 'shock' to the body. Intentional violence, accidents and surgical operations all have a profound effect on an individual. The ancient skull of Meryrahashetef at the British Museum is a clear case of trauma in ancient Egypt. On the left side of this adult male's head is a severe injury which, to judge from the lack of a healing response occurred not long before his death; and it is likely that the injury contributed to his death. According to an inscribed head rest found in his tomb, Meryrahashetef, who lived during the Sixth Dynasty, was an overseer of tenant farmers. His occupation reminds us that traumatic head injuries occur in domestic circumstances, and are not exclusively encountered in military action.

In plain terms, a fracture is a break in the structural continuity of a bone and any bone in the body could undergo such stress. Head (or cranial) injuries commonly occurred in most ancient populations, and not least in ancient Egypt and Nubia. Head injuries are particularly interesting in that they are more likely, but not always, the result of intentional violence. During G. Reisner's excavations at Kerma in Nubia it was noticed that many skulls from the site had deep depressions of various sizes on them. These injuries have been studied by J.M. Filer and their very nature suggests that they were intentionally inflicted. The depressions seem to have been made with a fairly blunt implement and it is not unlikely that some of the incidents occurred in domestic circumstances. An examination of extant examples of mallets and throwsticks reveals them to have been an ideal instrument for inflicting the Kerma injuries. Some might suggest that this evidence points to an argumentative community

53 *Skull of Meryrahashetef (Sixth Dynasty) with a fracture to the left side.*

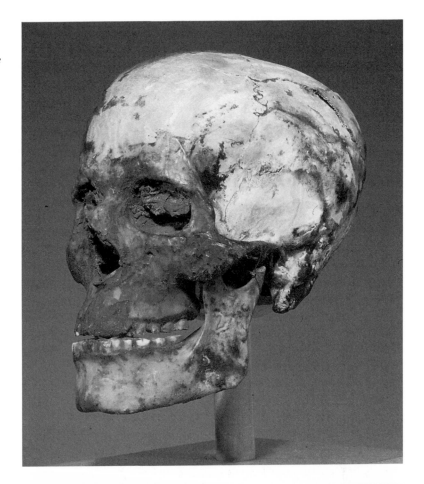

54 *Meryrahashetef: close-up of fracture on left parietal bone. No healing has taken place.*

which occasionally broke out into violent dispute. Interestingly most of the depressed injuries on the Kerma skulls had healed, leaving the recipients with little more than a smooth dent in the skull. Also of interest is the fact that almost as many women as men had one or more depressed cranial injuries.

In Egypt and Nubia, as in most other cultures, many more men than women sustained head injuries, most probably because men engaged more in military action and in the heavy manual work which could lead to lesions on the skull and other parts of the body. Furthermore, Egyptian soldiers tended not to wear helmets relying instead on the thickness of their hair as 'protection'. Many tomb scenes from ancient Egypt show men engaging in combat. It is important to note that the majority of the Egyptians in this scene are wielding weapons with their right hands and it is no coincidence that the majority of head injuries, including that of Meryrahashetef, occur on the left side of the head. These left-sided head injuries are consistent with a right-handed attacker if committing a frontal

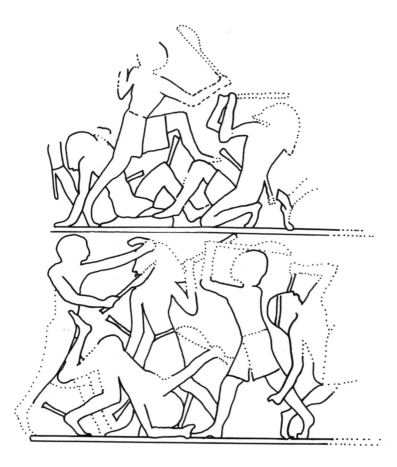

55 *Head injuries being inflicted in a fighting scene, tomb of Inti (Fifth Dynasty).*

assault. The fact that most of them seem to be inflicted by right-handed people is not surprising because, like more recent peoples, the ancient Egyptians actively discouraged left-handedness, viewing it as ill-omened. Of course, some injuries were sustained on the back and right side of the head, but they are in a minority.

In 1923, excavations at Deir el-Bahri near the Valley of the Kings unearthed a group of bodies (subsequently described in detail by H. E. Winlock in a roughly-hewn room. It was realised that the bodies, about sixty in number, were the remains of archers from the early Middle Kingdom, the end of a period of political upheaval in Egypt. No doubt these archers had played their part in the conflicts which ultimately led to peace. Many of them, some with older, healed wounds, had serious skull injuries consistent with being pierced by arrows or being hit by an axe or sword. Some of the wounds had been caused by rocks and stones being hurled down onto the men from above. Fifteen of the men had been clubbed repeatedly about the head, neck and face, and one archer had the weapon which caused his injury still in place: the wooden tip of an arrow was still embedded in his left eye socket, penetrating deeply into his skull. Had this man lived he would undoubtedly have lost the sight in that eye.

56 Severe injury on the frontal part of an Egyptian skull.

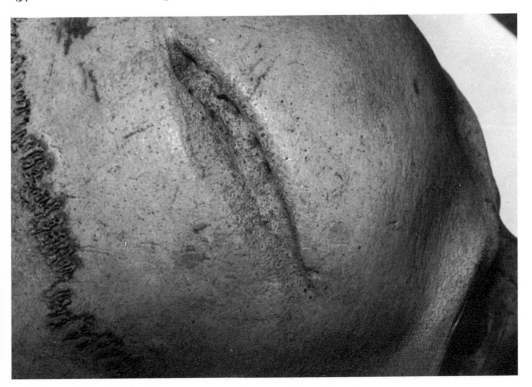

Not all head injuries are fatal and others reveal the effect they had on the recipient's life. A skull brought to England from Giza and now in Cambrdge has an extensive but well-healed injury to the left side of the head, running from the top of the skull down through the mastoid area. It is highly probable that as a result of his injury this adult male suffered a hearing loss. He may also have suffered bouts of dizziness due to damage of the middle ear, where the organs of balance are situated. It is a source of wonder that these ancient peoples survived such horrific cranial injuries without the aid of modern antibiotics.

Probably the most famous case of head injury is that of Seqenenre Tao, a king of the Seventeenth Dynasty who took part in the war to rid his country of its foreign rulers, the Hyksos. His mummified body, now in the Cairo Museum, has six wounds to the head, face and neck which were all made by weapons of a type used by the Hyksos. It was thought that all six injuries were inflicted on the battlefield and that the king died as a result of them. However, X-ray analysis of Seqenenre's skull by E. Metzel has shown that the bone around one of the wounds to the forehead had partially re-grown indicating that the king had sustained this injury some months before the others which killed him. It is possible that this first injury caused the paralysis evident in one of the king's arms. As an infirm individual he would surely not have returned to the battlefield and so the second and fatal set of injuries may have been sustained elsewhere. It has led to the suggestion that Seqenenre died as a result of a palace intrigue.

The Edwin Smith Surgical Papyrus, mentioned earlier, is an important source of information about head injuries. The description and suggested treatment of the lesions in this medical treatise show that the Egyptian doctor had extensive experience of head and facial damage. The text advises which injuries to treat (for example, a broken nose) and which to leave alone because there was no remedy available to the doctor.

Had the rest of the papyrus survived we would no doubt be better informed about treatment for injuries to other parts of the body. But without this information we can look to the bodies themselves for elucidation. Fractures of the post-cranial skeleton are quite numerous in mummies and skeletons and again, as with head injuries, they may tell us what people were doing when they received the injury. Fractures of the femur are common in ancient Egyptian human remains. A right femur in the British Museum has an obvious but well-healed break in the centre of the shaft. Whilst the two halves have successfully united under callus (a thick cuff of bone) and the join is perfectly strong, they are slightly misaligned. This means that this individual had one leg slightly shorter than the other and walked

57 *Head of King Seqenenre Tao (Seventeenth Dynasty) with severe wounds (top). One of these wounds may have caused the paralysis in his arm (below).*

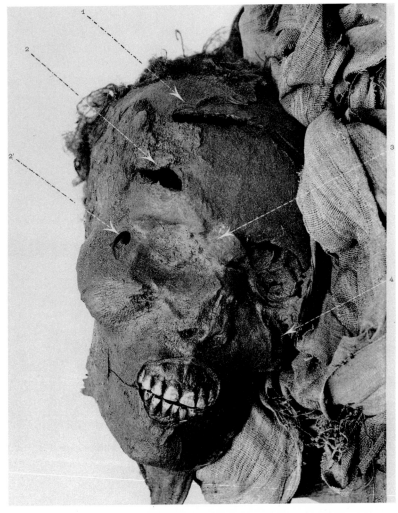

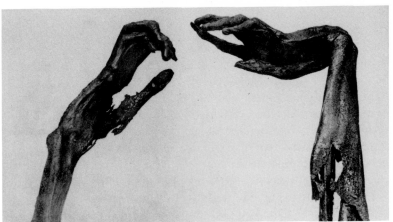

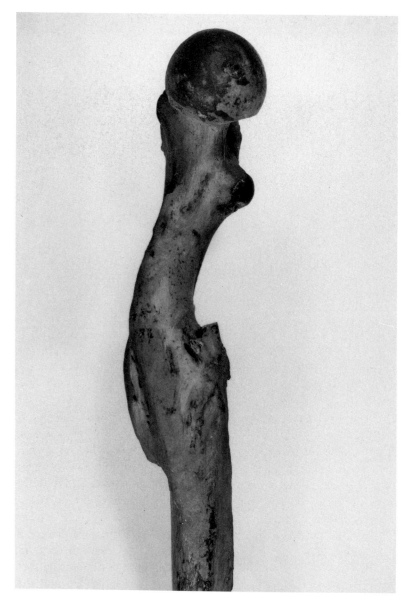

58 *A femur fractured midshaft and healed out of alignment. (New Kingdom date).*

with a limp. The long period of immobility whilst the leg set would have made the person dependant upon his community. X-ray studies of the Pharaoh Merenptah, who was over fifty when he assumed the throne, have revealed fractures in the heads of both femurs. This may have happened because he was elderly. This type of fracture is commonly seen today in elderly people after a fall.

It is interesting to note the pattern of fractures in different societies of the world. Whereas head injuries show remarkable homogeneity

59 *Splints (of palm tree ribs) supporting a broken arm bone. Nubian, Old Kingdom date.*

throughout the world this is not the case for fractures to other parts of the body. Comparisons between ancient Egypt and other ancient societies in America and Britain, for example, have shown that fractures of the radius and ulna (the forearm) were extremely common, reaching almost fifty per cent of a population group in some cases. The site of the fracture on these bones often gives a clue as to the cause of injury. Fractures in the central part of the forearm bones suggest an intentional blow as the arms are raised to parry or ward off an aggressive assault. The many examples of such parry fractures on female bodies in Nubian cemeteries led Elliot Smith to suggest that these were cases of flagrant wife beating! A recently discovered parry fracture of a right radius from Meroitic Gabati in Sudan does not fit in with Smith's idea as this broken arm bone belonged to a robust adult male (plate VIII). Injuries to the wrist area (a Colles' fracture) do not have such dramatic connotations as they are often the result of a fall onto the outstretched arm. Despite the aforementioned examples of fractured femurs such injuries were not as common as upper limb fractures in ancient Egyptian groups. It is suggested that the relatively low incidence of fractures to the tibia (shin bone) may be due to people going barefoot, especially when cultivating the land.

There is evidence that at least some form of treatment was attempted for these fractures. The Edwin Smith Surgical Papyrus suggests that the doctors of ancient Egypt had considerable knowledge of surgery. The recommended treatment for a fractured (or broken) nose was to insert rigid rolls of linen into the nostril like a splint. A number of long bones with splints attached to them have been found in graves, several of which come from the Old Kingdom period. Some splints were made from bark, others from bundles of wooden sticks tied together with cloth. Some splints included a padding of linen and vegetable fibre. A detail from a scene in the tomb of the sculptor Ipuy shows a man setting a dislocated shoulder, another form of trauma.

Amputation was a surgical procedure which had both punitive and therapeutic purposes. A battle scene on a royal mortuary temple wall from the Nineteenth Dynasty shows the number of enemy dead being calculated by the number of hands cut off. Diodorus Siculus wrote that amputation was imposed as a legal punishment in Egypt. Indeed a legal papyrus related that conspirators against the king had their noses and ears amputated. In a more therapeutic vein amputation could be performed to provide relief from an incurable condition, such as gangrene. A forearm of the Ninth Dynasty was amputated above the wrist during life and the two bones had become united by callus. A mummy from the Ptolemaic period with a forearm amputated during life had been fitted with a symbolic artificial limb during its embalming to ensure the person was given a new limb in the afterlife.

A surgical procedure which is not mentioned in medical texts and which is depicted only on two occasions is circumcision. The better-known scene is from the Sixth Dynasty tomb of Ankhmahor at Saqqara, and shows two young men being circumcised. The other scene, badly damaged, is in the Temple of Mut-en-Asheru at Karnak. An examination of mummies has shown that circumcision was frequently practised in ancient Egypt.

There is one surgical procedure which has never been adequately proven from pharaonic Egypt, that of trepanation (or trephining), the cutting (or scraping) and removal of pieces of bone from the skull to relieve pressure on the brain. In ancient times the procedure was likely to have been used either to treat head injuries or for magical practices, and it is still practised today in certain parts of the world, such as Kenya. There is striking evidence for the use of trepanation in other ancient cultures. A skull from Third Dynasty Tarkhan has thirteen small holes which were once thought to have been made before the patient had died, but are now thought to have been made after death. The Romans used this procedure, so it would not be unexpected to find Egyptian skulls of Roman date with trephine marks. One described by André Macke which has a circular groove may have been trepanned. An Egyptian skull from Giza, dating from 600–300 BC, has a large regularly shaped lesion which may have been trepanned and which shows some signs of new bone growth. Most important is the fact that this skull had received quite dramatic head injuries. In many societies, as already stated, trepanation was done to

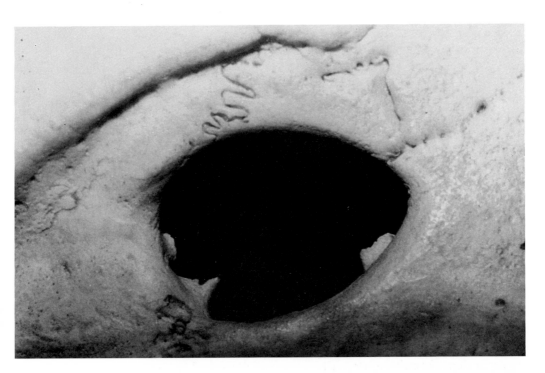

relieve pressure that can build up after a serious cranial lesion and it is not uncommon to find these two types of lesions together on the same skull. Yet despite the large numbers of pharaonic Egyptian and the many Nubian bodies which have been examined none have exhibited a burr-hole typical of unquestionable trepanation.

Artificial deformation is a traumatic (but not surgical) procedure, common to many societies but not to ancient Egypt. Many societies at different periods have sought to alter their appearance, particularly the shape of the head. Deformation of the skull by applying pressure from birth onwards is regarded in medical terms as a chronic low-grade trauma. The types of pressure vary according to the shape required. Some South American cultures wanting a flattened and foreshortened skull shape applied boards to the forehead and the back of the head. In other South American cultures, in Europe and in parts of Africa an elongated head was seen as desirable. To achieve this, bands were placed around the posterior part of the skull during the growing period to gradually press the skull into a longer shape. This procedure is still being practised in parts of Nigeria. Egyptologists have long speculated about the shape of the heads of the Amarna princesses, and that of their father the pharaoh Akhenaten. Several paintings and statues of these girls seem to indicate that they had exceptionally elongated heads, perhaps proof of artificial deformation being practised in ancient Egypt. The shape

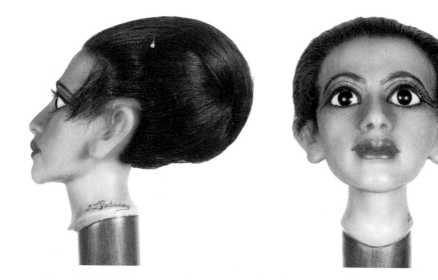

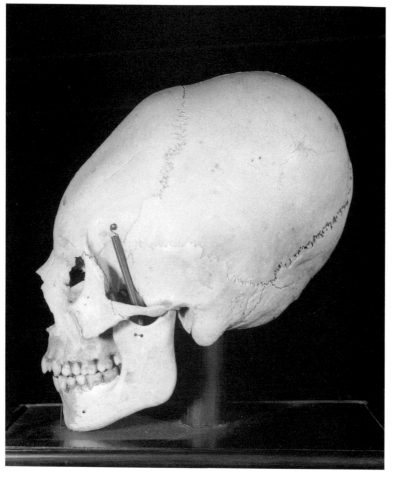

61, **62** *Front and side views of the wax model which may be a reconstruction of the skull below.*

63 *Skull, possibly from El Fashim (also known as the Medall skull), the shape of which appears to have been deliberately altered.*

of these representations of skulls can be viewed in two ways: that the girls' heads had been deliberately manipulated during infancy in order to reshape their skulls, or that the depictions conform to the prevailing artistic style of the Amarna period. At least one of the princesses (Ankhesenamun, who became the wife of Tutankhamun) and Akhenaten himself are depicted elsewhere with a normal skull shape which suggests the shape is largely a matter of artistic convention. Whichever view is taken, however, it must remain conjecture, for neither the bodies of the princesses nor those of their parents have been found. There is certainly no evidence from the Amarna period or any other period in Egyptian history to suggest that such a procedure was the norm. A skull of a young woman in the Royal College of Surgeons, London has also played its part in the speculation as to whether or not ancient Egyptians practised cranial deformation. The skull's provenance and age is uncertain but is thought to have come from a Coptic cemetery at El Fashim dating to between the first and sixth centuries AD. It is also uncertain whether or not a small modern wax model with the skull was intended as a reconstruction of it. The skull is certainly elongated, and this may be the result of deliberate deformation, but as the skull is surrounded by so many uncertainties, no firm conclusions can be drawn from it.

CHAPTER SEVEN

Dental Health

Extremely worn teeth, dental abscesses and advanced periodontal disease affecting the gums and bones – a nightmare catalogue of dental problems. Such a picture of poor dental health might be assumed to be that of a poor and inadequately nourished Egyptian peasant but, in fact, this is a picture of the state of dental health of the royal mummy which has been identified as Amenhotep III, one of the greatest of the Egyptian pharaohs. According to James Harris and Kent Weeks who examined the bodies of ancient Egyptian royalty, many of them, including Ramesses II, Yuya, Thuya and Merenptah, had appalling dentitions. By contrast the predynastic body at the British Museum known as Ginger, who lived in a much less luxurious society, had fairly healthy teeth. Of the many thousands of mummies and skeletons examined, the majority exhibit some form of dental pathology. Dental disease is an acquired disorder but it is such an important topic in the study of ancient Egyptian and Nubian remains that it merits a chapter of its own. Evidence of dental disease is very plentiful because teeth generally survive very well, and are often the best preserved parts of a body. They are often less affected by the ravages of climate, and may survive better than the bones of the skeleton in more acidic soils.

Worn teeth like those of Amenhotep III are a common finding in ancient Egyptian dentitions. Teeth are actually meant to be worn down and this occurs as the crowns of the teeth are ground against one another. In daily life any abrasive particles in food inevitably wear down the biting surfaces of teeth as the food is processed between them. Collagen in meats, cellulose and silica structures in plants, and grit in stone-ground flour may all contribute to the wearing down of tooth surfaces.

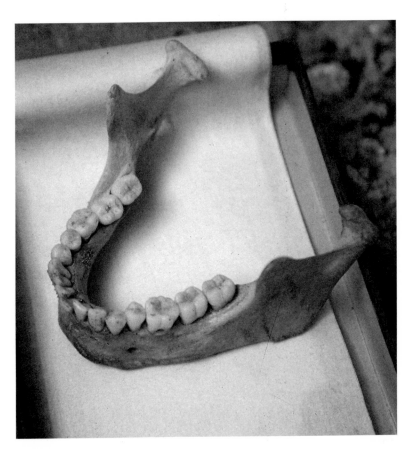

This wearing down process is called attrition and is clearly distinct from abrasion or scratches on the teeth. Attrition denotes well-defined wear on the biting surface of the teeth and is related to the movements of the jaw during chewing, whereas abrasion is a more diffuse wear featuring randomly orientated scorings on areas of the tooth other than the biting surfaces. Dental attrition in itself is not a pathological condition but in severe cases it may lead to, or encourage, other serious dental problems, by allowing bacteria to gain access to the interior of the tooth. Some of these problems will be described in the course of this chapter. Attrition has been noted, particularly in ancient Egyptian and Nubian dentitions, where it is concentrated on the molar (or back) teeth. Filce Leek, a dentist who studied the dental health of many ancient Egyptians, analysed samples of ancient bread and found that the bread contained varying amounts of contaminants, largely sand and grit, which could have been accidentally introduced during the different stages of bread production. The action of winnowing and sifting grain may not have sufficiently removed sand particles, and specks of stone could have

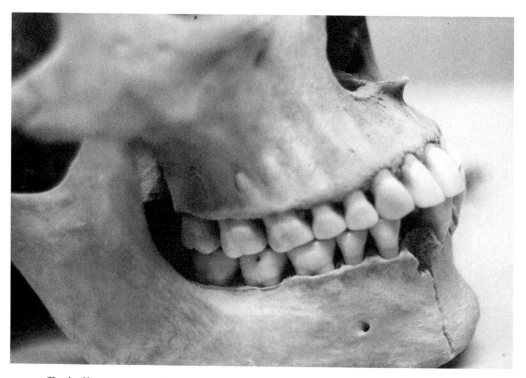

worn off grinding querns and been incorporated into the flour during the grinding process. Pliny and other classical authors have referred to the custom of adding sand or powdered brick to grain to facilitate its grinding. Recent attempts to replicate ancient grinding methods using querns and ancient strains of grain have shown that the introduction of a gritty substance into the grain would have in fact aided the crushing of hard and compact husks. Leek concluded, therefore, that the grit in Egyptian bread, whether deliberately or accidentally introduced, caused attrition. This suggestion is reasonable if the bread analysed is known to have been for domestic consumption. However, it is possible that the samples analysed by Leek were funerary ones and so were likely to have been roughly made, not being meant for actual consumption. C. Duhig believes that the attrition on ancient Egyptian teeth, which is exceptional even for the ancient world, must have another cause. She is re-examining tooth surfaces microscopically to identify the attritional agents.

There are two main forms of dental disease: periodontal disease which affects the gums and jaw bones, and dental caries. Both of these conditions are related to the formation of plaque on the teeth. Plaque is a sticky film on the teeth in which bacteria proliferate. Plaque irritates the gums causing gingivitis, an inflammation of the gums, which is the first stage of periodontal disease. If this gingivitis

65 Caries seem to have been a rare occurrence throughout pharaonic history. However, a carious lesion can be seen on a right molar on this Old Kingdom skull from Mostagedda.

66 *Mandible with an abscess destroying a tooth socket.*

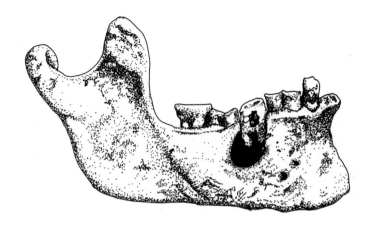

remains unchecked, then the inflammation continues down into the root of the tooth destroying fibres which hold the tooth in its socket and eventually the tooth falls out, or is removed. In extreme cases the actual bone of the jaw can be infected and start decaying. Periodontal disease affects mostly the molar teeth, probably because they are less readily cleaned by the action of the tongue and saliva when eating and speaking. Diet obviously must play an important role in the cause of periodontal disease as foodstuffs containing sugars and carbohydrates will promote a rapid growth of plaque. Vitamin D deficiency produces swelling and bleeding of the gums and so may also result in periodontal disease. It has been suggested that psychological stress – often undervalued in archaeological contexts, as it cannot be detected – may also promote soft tissue infections. Overall, periodontal disease points to dietary deficiencies, poor oral hygiene and periods of stress and illness, all of which may indicate the quality of life for ancient Egyptians, and ancient populations generally.

Plaque also plays its part in the process of dental caries, more commonly known as tooth decay, which if left untreated can also lead to the loss of the infected tooth through the formation of an abscess. Some of the bacteria (streptococcus mutans) in plaque change sugar into acid, which then attacks the tooth surface. The acid eats into the enamel causing decay inside the tooth. The situation is worsened when any plaque not removed calcifies to form calculus (or tartar) which creates pockets where decay can be intensified. The decay continues into the dentine where it can progress quite quickly, the dentine being less tough than enamel. Continuing its journey the decay enters the pulp chamber and here may affect the nerves to the tooth. Decay spreading unchecked throughout the root may eventually spread into the bony socket creating a dental abscess. This pus-filled cavity then bursts through the bone to release the pus. Often the affected tooth cannot recover and is lost. During life the empty socket will gradually be resorbed resulting in a smooth contour. It is not unusual in archaeological material to find totally endentulous jaw bones. Dental caries occur more commonly on the biting surfaces of the teeth, but may occur between teeth. Again, it is the molar teeth which are more greatly affected by caries and abscesses. Many studies show that dental caries were fairly rare in ancient Egypt and that the rate of caries increased slowly from predynastic to dynastic periods, reaching the highest levels during the Roman period and afterwards. As dental caries is associated with diet, this may be an indication of a gradual swing towards a sugar- and carbohydrate-laden diet during the Graeco-Roman periods. Dental abscesses can occur when particles of food are jammed between teeth and forced into the root of the tooth, the resulting decay causing an abscess. Dental abscesses are more commonly found in the molar region of the dentition and occurred frequently in the ancient world. Of the many collections of Egyptian and Nubian skeletal and mummified remains, there cannot be many without at least one example of a dental abscess. Certainly the royal personages mentioned at the beginning of this chapter suffered from them as did Horemkenesi, the Bristol mummy, who had two abscesses in his upper jaw. Several excellent examples of dental abscesses were found during the recent excavations at Gabati in Central Sudan.

As teeth develop a number of problems can occur, one of which is imperfect production of enamel, the hard outer surface of teeth. Hypoplasia, one of the forms of imperfectly formed enamel, is particularly relevant to the study of ancient health patterns. Hypoplasia is probably the most commonly found dental condition from antiquity and its occurrence is related to the way teeth are formed. The enamel covering of a tooth is made up of 'sleeves' which overlap. Normally these 'sleeves' develop steadily but sometimes this continuity can be interrupted causing a 'jump' or a ridge in the smooth enamel surface. Thus the surface contour of the tooth is changed and this can be discovered visually or detected with the aid of a dental probe. A defective diet has been viewed as one possible cause of hypoplastic lines. Dr S. Hillson, of the Institute of Archaeology in London, studied the dentitions of groups of skeletons from Badari, Sedment and Hawara. He found a high incidence of hypoplasia in the three- to five-year-old children in these groups, suggesting that these youngsters had undergone some form of dietary stress during their short life. Modern studies have also shown that children develop hypoplastic lines as a response to severe malnutrition. It has also been suggested that hypoplastic grooves are formed after illnesses, especially febrile ones, and that the occurrence of tetanus, generalised gut infections, some endocrine disorders and many childhood diseases may be reflected in hypoplastic lesions. A single band of

67 *A skeleton from Gabati, Sudan (post-Meroitic period) revealing a fairly healthy dentition.*

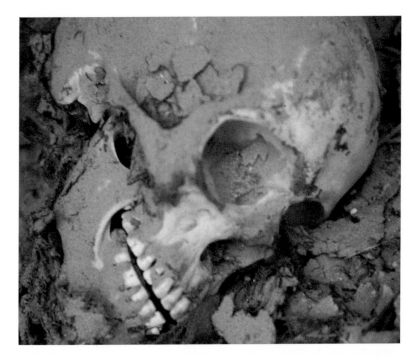

hypoplasia represents one anomalous event in the development of that tooth's enamel, multiple grooves indicate a series of developmental disturbances. As hypoplasia may occur in conjunction with other indicators of stress, such as lines of arrested growth in the long bones and pitting in the eye sockets, useful information can be deduced about any environmental stress, including illness and poor diet, during an individual's childhood. As teeth develop at different rates, those showing signs of hypoplasia can be compared in order to build up a picture of an individual's life. This information in turn can be used on a wider scale to assess the effect of environmental stress at a population level.

In Chapter 4 the skeleton of a child with the disorder osteogenesis imperfecta was discussed. In addition to the skeletal problems, the child's teeth have also developed abnormally. The teeth are brittle and discoloured and have poorly developed roots.

Occlusion is the term which denotes the position of the teeth when the jaws are brought together, and in normal development it is usual for the upper, or maxillary teeth, to hang over the lower, or mandibular teeth. The habit of thumb sucking or pushing the tongue forward may, however, result in markedly protruding upper teeth, a condition commonly known as buck teeth, and this type of malocclusion was observed by James Harris when he examined the dentitions of thousands of modern Nubian children. It is thought that there is a tendency for malocclusion to run in families and so it can be used to suggest a close family relationship between individuals. This was the case with members of Egypt's Seventeenth Dynasty royal family. X-rays of a disarticulated head believed to be that of Tetisheri, wife of Senakhtenre Tao, reveal markedly protruding upper teeth, a strong trait which is seen in the dental X-rays of Ahmose-Nefertary, wife of Ahmose I, who was Tetisheri's grand-daughter.

Any discussion of dental health will inevitably lead to the question of whether or not the ancient Egyptians attempted dental surgery. The subject has been one of great controversy, although the 'debate' has involved only a few specimens. In 1917, E. A. Hooton wrote 'the evidence of this specimen seems to establish beyond a reasonable doubt the existence of a rudimentary knowledge of oral surgery in the Old Empire'. The specimen he was referring to was a mandible (lower jaw) of Old Kingdom date from Giza, which exhibited two round holes near the right first molar. The perfect symmetry of the holes led Hooton to believe that they had been drilled by an ancient Egyptian dentist to relieve a painful abscess. What Hooton did not take into account was the fact that an abscess will often create its own pathway through the jaw-bone in order to evacuate pus, the resulting sinus (cavity in bone) usually looking remarkably circular and precise. In his publication of the Edwin Smith Papyrus, J. H. Breasted also suggested the abscesses in the jaw of a Twelfth Dynasty skull had been treated by drilling into the bone. Breasted's comments were no doubt prompted by H. Junker's publication in 1929 of what seemed to be proof of a dental profession in ancient Egypt. The 'proof' consisted of two molar teeth, linked together by gold wire, which were found by Junker in shaft 984 of a mastaba tomb at Giza.

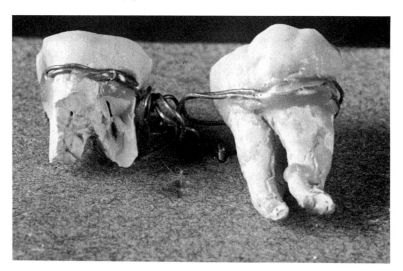

68 *Two molar teeth found by Junker (originally joined by gold wire) and the cause of much controversy.*

Originally Junker had thought the device had been constructed for use during the mummification process and it was not until a specialist declared the device to be the work of a highly skilled ancient practitioner, that the idea of its being an ancient prosthetic device was born. Many years later the teeth, now separated from the gold wire, were examined by Filce Leek, a dentist well acquainted with ancient Egyptian teeth. Leek was quite adamant in his assertions that the device could not have been used during life. He felt the loops of gold wire insufficient to hold the two teeth within a living, and therefore masticating, mouth. It was also stressed that the teeth were not found within an oral cavity, but in rubble lying around the skeleton. Furthermore, layers of a hardened substance on the teeth were not positively identified as calculus (tartar), which would have indicated use in a living individual; instead Leek thought that this represented the result of action of the minerals (in the rubble) upon the gold.

In an interesting codicil to the controversy, Dr Michael Schulz of Göttingen University has recently proposed that the two molars under discussion are not even from the same original dentition and he is currently examining the teeth microscopically to determine this question.

A carved wooden panel for Hesyre of the Third Dynasty accords him a dentistry title and other sources show that pharmaceutical remedies were available to help those suffering from dental disease. The Ebers Papyrus has two prescriptions 'to expel an eating ulcer (that is an abscess) from the gums'. One prescription called for cumin, colocynth and terebinth. This mixture may have provided temporary relief from pain as colocynth (bitter apple) is a cathartic, and terebinth (turpentine) has antiseptic properties. In the twentieth century terebinth has been used as a medicine in linament form. The second prescription contained cow's milk, earth almonds and 'evening dew'. It is possible that cinnamon, having mildly astringent properties, was also used rather like cloves as an antiseptic mouth-wash and for toothache. Judging from ritual evidence the King's oral hygiene included chewing natron, to purify his mouth, as part of his morning toilet.

Teeth differ from bones in their biological make-up and may sometimes yield more information about an individual's health than the skeleton. Teeth have a fair degree of variation in their shape and are often more easily identifiable, even in a crushed state, than bones in the same condition. Teeth are dimorphic, that is they occur in two gender-related forms and so health comparisons can be made between the males and females in a population group. Importantly, teeth record their response to aspects of the environment such as diet and illness, and so are valuable indicators of environmental change. As dental pathology is fairly common and readily diagnosed, the resulting statistics on its different forms are also a useful tool for comparing human groups or populations.

Chronological Table

PREDYNASTIC PERIODS
*c.*4500–3000 BC

EARLY DYNASTIC
Dynasties 1–3
*c.*3100–2613 BC

OLD KINGDOM
Dynasties 4–8
*c.*2613–2160 BC

FIRST INTERMEDIATE PERIOD
Dynasties 9–10 and Dynasty 11
in southern Upper Egypt
*c.*2160–2025 BC

MIDDLE KINGDOM
Dynasties 11–13 over all Egypt
*c.*2025–1700 BC

SECOND INTERMEDIATE PERIOD
Dynasty 13 over Upper Egypt
and Dynasties 14–17
*c.*1700–1550 BC

NEW KINGDOM
Dynasty 18
*c.*1550–1295 BC
Dynasty 19
*c.*1295–1186 BC
Dynasty 20
*c.*1186–1069 BC

THIRD INTERMEDIATE PERIOD
Dynasty 21
*c.*1069–945 BC
Dynasties 22–23
*c.*945–727 BC

LATE PERIOD
Dynasties 24–30 and Persian
occupation
*c.*727–332 BC

PTOLEMAIC PERIOD
332–30 BC

ROMAN PERIOD
30 BC–AD 330

BYZANTINE PERIOD
AD 330–641

ISLAMIC PERIOD
After AD 641

Illustration Acknowledgements

Abbreviation:
BM: By courtesy of the Trustees of the British Museum

Front cover: BM (EA 41603)
Frontispiece: R. Connolly/R. Read, Department of Human Anatomy and Cell Biology, University of Liverpool

1 Graham Harrison.
2 Drawing by Neville Parker.
3 Joann Fletcher.
4 Drawing by Neville Parker.
5 Drawing by Neville Parker.
6 Drawing by Neville Parker.
7 Joyce M. Filer.
8 Joyce M. Filer.
9 Joyce M. Filer.
10 BM (Soba, Z3, 177).
11 Drawing by Neville Parker.
12 Drawing by Neville Parker.
13 Drawing by Richard Parkinson.
14 Carol Andrews.
15 BM (EA 10686).
16 Geoffrey T. Martin.
17 Manchester Museum.
18 Jonathan Musgrave.
19 BM (EA 52921).
20 Institute of Archaeology, London.
21 Stephen Hughes.
22 Rodney Reznek.
23 Jonathan Musgrave.
24 Joann Fletcher.
25 Royal College of Surgeons, Hunterian Museum.
26 Royal College of Surgeons, Hunterian Museum.
27 Griffith Institute, Oxford.
28 BM (EA 60131).
29 *Left*: BM (Soba, Z3, 270).
Right: Institute of Archaeology, London.
30 Joyce M. Filer.
31 Joyce M. Filer.
32 Drawing by Neville Parker.
33 Drawing by Neville Parker.
34 Drawing by Christine Barratt (after original in situ)
35 BM (EA 74106).
36 R. Connolly/R. Read, Department of Human Anatomy and Cell Biology, University of Liverpool.
37 R. Connolly/R. Read, Department of Human Anatomy and Cell Biology, University of Liverpool.
38 Drawing by Neville Parker.
39 Drawing by Neville Parker.
40 Drawing by Neville Parker.
41 Bolton Museum and Art Gallery.
42 Bolton Museum and Art Gallery.
43 Joyce M. Filer.
44 From G. Elliot Smith and W. R. Dawson, *Egyptian Mummies* (London, 1924) fig. 62.
45 Drawing by Neville Parker.
46 From G. Elliot Smith and W. R. Dawson, *Egyptian Mummies* (London, 1924) fig. 66.
47 Drawing by Richard Parkinson.
48 BM (EA 562).

49 From G. Elliot Smith and W. R. Dawson, *Egyptian Mummies* (London, 1924) fig. 64.

50 Joyce M. Filer.

51 Joyce M. Filer.

52 Joyce M. Filer.

53 BM (EA 55725).

54 BM (EA 55725).

55 Drawing by Neville Parker.

56 Joyce M. Filer.

57 From G. Elliot Smith, *The Royal Mummies* (Catalogue Général du Musée du Caire), (Cairo, 1912), pls I and II.

58 BM (EA 37340).

59 Royal College of Surgeons, Hunterian Museum.

60 Joyce M. Filer.

61 Royal College of Surgeons, Hunterian Museum.

62 Royal College of Surgeons, Hunterian Museum.

63 Royal College of Surgeons, Hunterian Museum.

64 Joyce M. Filer.

65 Joyce M. Filer.

66 Drawing by Neville Parker.

67 Joyce M. Filer.

68 Heidesheim, Pelizaeus-Museum, inv. no. 2453.

Colour Plates

  I. BM (EA 32753).

 II. Egypt Exploration Society.

III. Joyce M. Filer.

IV. The Leicester Galleries, London

 V. Reg Davis.

VI. BM (EA 41603).

VII. Joyce M. Filer.

VIII. BM (Gabati T68, skeleton 118).

Bibliography

Andrews, C., *Egyptian Mummies*, (London, 1984).

Armelagos, G., Jacobs, K. H., and Martin, D. L., 'Death and Demography in Prehistoric Sudanese Nubia', *Mortality and Immortality: the anthropology and archaeology of death*. Proceedings of a meeting of the Research Seminar in Archaeology and Related Subjects held at the Institute of Archaeology, London University, in June 1980 (London, 1981), 33–57.

Bierbrier, M. L., *The Tomb-builders of the Pharaohs* (London, 1982).

Breasted, J. H., *The Edwin Smith Surgical Papyrus* (Chicago, 1930).

Brothwell, D., and Sandison, A. T., *Diseases in Antiquity* (Springfield, Illinois, 1967).

Butzer, K., *Early Hydraulic Civilisation in Egypt* (Chicago, 1976).

Cockburn, A., and Cockburn, E. (eds), *Mummies, Disease and Ancient Cultures* (Cambridge, 1980).

Dasen, V., *Dwarfs in Ancient Egypt and Greece* (Oxford, 1993).

David, R., *Mysteries of the Mummies* (London, 1978).

David, A. R., and Tapp, E. (eds), *Evidence Embalmed* (Manchester, 1982).

David, A. R., (ed.) *Science in Egyptology* (Manchester, 1986).

David, A. R., and Tapp, E. (eds), *The Mummy's Tale* (London, 1992).

Davies, W. V. and Walker, R., (eds), *Biological Anthropology and the Study of Ancient Egypt*, (London, 1993).

Dawson, W. R. and Gray, P. H. K., *Catalogue of Egyptian Antiquities in the British Museum I: Mummies and Human Remains* (London, 1968).

Dawson, W. R., 'Pygmies and Dwarfs In Ancient Egypt', *Journal of Egyptian Archaeology*, 24, (1938), 185–9.

Derry, D. E., 'A Case of Hydrocephalus In An Egyptian Of The Roman Period', *Journal of Anatomy and Physiology*, 47, Third Series, vol. VIII, Fourth Part (July 1913), 436–58.

Diodorus Siculus, Oldfather, C. H. (transl.) reprint (London, 1979).

Dobson, J., 'A Curator's Curiosity', *Annals of the Royal College of Surgeons*, 24 (1959), 331–37.

Dols, M. (ed.), *Medieval Islamic Medicine, Ibn Ridwan's Treatise 'On the Prevention of Bodily Ills in Egypt'*. (California, 1984).

Duhig, C., 'Reconsideration of the cause of severe attrition in ancient Egyptian teeth', *Homo*, vol. 45 Suppl., Special issue Xth European Meeting of the Paleopathology Association, Gottingen, 29th–3rd September (1994), S41.

Dzierzykray-Rogalsky, T., 'Paleopathology of the Ptolemaic Inhabitants of Dakhleh Oasis (Egypt)', *Journal of Human Evolution*, 9 (1980), 71–74.

Filer, J. M., 'Head Injuries in Egypt and Nubia: a comparison of skulls from Giza and Kerma', *Journal of Egyptian Archaeology*, 78, (1992), 281–85.

Filer, J. M., 'The SARS excavations at Gabati, Central Sudan, 1994–5: C: The Skeleton Remains', *The Sudan Archaeological Research Society Newsletter*, No. 8 (1995), 23–7.

Filer, J. M., 'Ancient Egypt as a source of information for cranial injuries' in J. Carman (ed.) *Material Harm: Studies in the Archaeology of War and Violence*, Worldwide Archaeology Series, Cruithne Press (in press).

Fletcher, J., 'A Tale of Hair, Wigs and Lice', *Egyptian Archaeology*, 5 (1994), 31–33.

Ghalioungui, P., *Magic and Medical Science in Ancient Egypt* (London, 1963).

Granville, A., 'An Essay on Egyptian Mummies; with observations on the art of embalming among the ancient Egyptians', *Philosophical Transactions of the Royal Society* (1825), 269–316.

Gray, P. H. K., 'A Case of Osteogenesis Imperfecta, Associated With Dentinogenesis Imperfecta, Dating From Antiquity', *Clinical Radiology*, 20 (1969), 106–8.

Harris, J. E. and Weeks, K. R., *X-Raying The Pharaohs* (London, 1973).

Harris, J. E. and Wente, E. F. (eds) *An X-Ray Atlas of the Royal Mummies* (Chicago, 1980).

Harrison, R. G., Connolly, R. C., Ahmed, S., Abdalla, A. B. and El Ghawaby, M., 'A Mummified Foetus From the Tomb of Tutankhamun', *Antiquity*, 53 (1979), 19–21 & pl.VIII.

Herodotus. Godley, A. D. (transl.), (London, 1920).

Hillson, S. W., 'Diet and Dental Disease', *World Archaeology*, vol. II, 147–62.

Hooton, E. A., 'Oral Surgery In Egypt During The Old Empire', in Bates, O. (ed.), *Harvard African Studies* I, Varia Africana I (Cambridge, Massachusetts), 1917, 29–32 & pls. I & II.

Leek, F. F., 'Teeth and Bread in Ancient Egypt', *Journal of Egyptian Archaeology*, 58 (1972), 253–90.

Manchester, K., *The Archaeology of Disease* (University of Bradford, 1983).

Miller, R. L. *et al*, 'Diagnosis of *Plasmodium falciparum* infections in mummies using the rapid manual *ParaSight*™-F test' *Transactions of the Royal Society of Tropical Medicine and Hygiene*, 88 (1994), 31–2.

Møller-Christensen, V. and Hughes, D. R., 'An Early Case of Leprosy from Nubia', *Man*, vol. 1, no. 2 June 1966, 242–3 and pls. 3a, 3b, 4a and 4b.

Moodie, R. L., *Roentgenologic Studies of Egyptian and Peruvian Mummies*, Field Museum of Natural History, Anthropology Memoirs vol. I & II (Chicago, 1931).

Nunn, John, *Ancient Egyptian Medicine*, London (in press).

Pettigrew, T. J., *A History of Egyptian Mummies* (London, 1834).

Podzorski, P., *Their Bones Shall Not Perish, An Examination of Predynastic Human Skeletal Remains from Naga-ed-Der in Egypt* (SIA Publishing, 1990).

Ruffer, M. A., *Studies In The Palaeopathology of Egypt* (Chicago, 1921).

Smith, G. Elliot, 'The Most Ancient Splints', *British Medical Journal*, 28 March (1906), 3–17.

Smith, G. Elliot and Jones, F. Wood, *The Archaeological Survey of Nubia*, Report for 1907–1908, vol. II; Report on the Human Remains (Cairo, 1910).

Smith, G. Elliot, *The Royal Mummies (Catalogue Général du Musée du Caire)* (Cairo, 1912).

Smith, G. Elliot and Dawson, W. R., *Egyptian Mummies* (London, 1924).

Strouhal, E., *Life in Ancient Egypt* (Cambridge, 1992).

Taylor, J. H., *Unwrapping A Mummy* (London, 1995).

Walker, R., 'Skeletal Remains', in Raven, M. J. (ed.) *The Tomb of Iurudef, a Memphite Official in the Reign of Ramesses II* (London, 1991), 55–76.

Winlock, H. E., *The Slain Soldiers of Neb-Hepet-Re Mentu-Hotpe* (The Metropolitan Museum of Art, 1945).

Index

Roman numerals in **bold** refer to colour plates. Arabic numerals in **bold** refer to black and white figures.